AF498393

The Old Coast Road

From Boston to Plymouth

Agnes Rothery

Originally Published by
HOUGHTON MIFFLIN COMPANY
1920

Contents

CHAPTER X   **83**

CHAPTER XI   **91**

BOSTON: A FOREWORD

To love Boston or to laugh at Boston—it all depends on whether or not you are a Bostonian. Perhaps the happiest attitude—and the most intelligent—is tinged with both amusement and affection: amusement at the undeviating ceremonial of baked beans on Saturday night and fish balls on Sunday morning; at the Boston bag (not so ubiquitous now as formerly); at the indefatigable consumption of lectures; at the Bostonese pronunciation; affection for the honorable traditions, noble buildings, distinguished men and women. Boston is an old city—one must remember that it was settled almost three centuries ago—and old cities, like old people, become tenacious of their idiosyncrasies, admitting their inconsistencies and prejudices with complacency, wisely aware that age has bestowed on them a special value, which is automatically increased with the passage of time.

To tell the story of an old city is like cutting down through the various layers of a fruity layer cake. When you turn the slice over, you see that every piece is a cross-section. So almost every locality and phase of this venerable metropolis could be studied, and really should be studied, according to its historical strata: Colonial, Provincial, Revolutionary, economic, and literary. All of these periods have piled up their associations one upon the other, and all of them must be somewhat understood if one would sincerely comprehend what has aptly been called not a city, but a "state of mind."

It is as impossible for the casual sojourner to grasp the significance of the multifarious historical and literary events which have transpired here as for a few pages to outline them. Wherever one stands in Boston suggests the church of San Clemente in Rome, where, you remember, there are three churches built one upon the other. However, those who would take the lovely journey from Boston to Plymouth needs must make some survey, no matter how superficial, of their starting-place. And perhaps the best spot from which to begin is the Common.

This pleasantly rolling expanse, which was set aside as long ago as 1640, with the decree that "there shall be no land granted either for houseplott or garden out of yͤe open land or common field," has been unbrokenly maintained ever since, and as far as acreage goes (it approximates fifty acres) could still fulfill its original use of pasturing cows, a practice which was continued until 1830. It was here that John Hancock's cattle grazed—he who lived in such magnificence on the hill, and in whose side yard the State House was built—and once, when preparations for an official banquet were halted by shortage of milk, tradition has it that he ordered his servants to hasten out on the Common and milk every cow there, regardless of ownership. Tradition also tells us that the little boy Ralph Waldo Emerson tended his mother's cow here; and finally both traditions and existing law declare that yonder one-story building opening upon Mount Vernon Street, and possessing an oddly wide door, must forever keep that door of sufficient width to let the cows pass through to the Common.

Let us stand upon the steps of the State House and look out over the Common. To our right, near the intersection of Boylston and Tremont Streets, lies the half-forgotten, almost obliterated Central Burying Ground, the final resting-place of Gilbert Stuart, the famous American painter. At the left points the spire of Park Street Church, notable not for its age, for it is only a little over a century old, but for its charming beauty, and by the fact that William Lloyd Garrison delivered his first address here, and here "America" was sung in public for the first time. It was the windiness of this corner which was responsible for Tom Appleton's suggestion (he was the brother-in-law of Longfellow) that a shorn lamb be tethered here.

The graceful spire of Park Street Church serves not only as a landmark, but is also a most fitting terminal to a street of many associations. It is on Park Street that the publishing house of Houghton, Mifflin & Co. (now Houghton Mifflin Company) has had its offices for forty years, and the bookstores and the antique shops tucked quaintly down a few steps below the level of the sidewalk have much of the flavor of a bit of London.

Still standing on the State House steps, facing the Common, you are also facing what has been called the noblest monument in Boston and the most successfully placed one in America. It is Saint-Gaudens's bronze relief of Colonel Robert G. Shaw commanding his colored regiment, and if you see no other sculpture in a city which has its full quota you must see this memorial, spirited in execution, spiritual in its conception of a mighty moment.

If we had time to linger we could not do better than to follow Beacon Street to the left, pausing at the Athenæum, a library of such dignity and beauty that one instinctively, and properly, thinks of it as an institution rather than a mere building. To enjoy the Athenæum one must be a "proprietor" and own a "share," which entitles one not only to the use of the scholarly volumes in scholarly seclusion, but also in the afternoon to entrance to an alcove where tea is served for three pennies. Perhaps here, as well as any other place, you may see a characteristic assortment of what are fondly called "Boston types." There is the professor from Cambridge, a gentleman with a pointed beard and a noticeably cultivated enunciation; one from Wellesley— this, a lady—with that keen and paradoxically impractical expression which marks pure intellectuality; an alert matron, plainly, almost shabbily, dressed (aristocratic Boston still scorns sartorial smartness); a very well-bred young girl with bone spectacles; a student, shabby, like the Back Bay matron, but for another reason; a writer; a business man whose hobby is Washingtonia. These, all of them, you may enjoy along with your cup of tea for three cents, if—and here is the crux—you can only be admitted in the first place. And if you are admitted, do not fail to look out of the rear windows upon the ancient Granary Burying Ground, where rest the ashes of Hancock, Sewall, Faneuil, Samuel Adams, Otis, Revere, and many more notables. If you have a penchant for graveyards, this one, entered from Tremont Street, is more than worthy of further study.

This is one of the many things we could enjoyably do if we had time, but whether we have time or not we must pay our respects to the State House (one does not call it the Capitol in Boston, as in other cities), the prominence of whose golden dome is not unsuggestive, to those who recall it, of Saint Botolph's beacon tower in Boston, England, for which this city was named. The State House is a distinctively American building, and Bulfinch, the great American architect, did an excellent thing when he designed it. The dome was originally covered with plates of copper rolled by no other than that expert silversmith and robust patriot, Paul Revere—he whose midnight ride has been recited by so many generations of school-children, and whose exquisite flagons, cups, ladles, and sugar tongs not only compared with the best Continental work of that period, but have set a name and standard for American craftsmanship ever since.

If you should walk up and down the chessboard of Beacon Hill—taking the knight's move occasionally across the narrow cross-streets—you could not help treading the very squares which were familiar to the feet of that generation of authors which has permanently stamped American literature. At 55 Beacon Street, down near the foot of the hill and facing the Common, still stands the handsome, swell-front, buff-brick house where Prescott, the historian, lived. On Mount Vernon Street (which runs parallel to Beacon, and which, with its dignified beauty, won the approval of that connoisseur of beautiful streets—Henry James) one can pick out successively the numbers 59, 76, 83, 84, the first and last being homes of Thomas Bailey Aldrich, and the other two distinguished by the residence of William Ellery Channing and Margaret Deland. Pinckney Street runs parallel with Mount Vernon, and the small, narrow house at number 20 was one of the homes of the Alcott family. It seems delightfully fitting that Louisburg Square—that very exclusive and very English spot which probably retains more of the quaint atmosphere and customs of an aristocratic past than any other single area in the city—should have been the home of the well-beloved William Dean Howells. One also likes to recall that Jenny Lind was married at number 20. Chestnut Street—which after a period of social obscurity is again coming into its own—possesses Julia Ward Howe's house at number 13, that of Motley the historian at 16, and of Parkman at 50. In this hasty map we have gone up and down the hill, but the cross-street, Charles, although not so attractive, is nevertheless as rich in literary associations as any in Boston. Here lived, for a short time, at 164, Oliver Wendell Holmes, and at 131—also for a short time—Thomas Bailey Aldrich. It is, however, at 148, that we should longest pause. This, for many rich years, was the home of James T. Fields, that delightful man of letters who was the friend of many men of letters; he who entertained Dickens and Thackeray, and practically every foreign writer of note who visited this country; he who encouraged Hawthorne to the completion of the "Scarlet Letter," and he, who, as an appreciative critic, publisher, and editor, probably did more to elevate, inspire, and sustain the general literary tone of the city than any other single person. In these stirring days facile American genius springs up, like brush fires, from coast to coast. Novels pour in from the West, the Middle West, the South. To superficial outsiders it may seem as if Boston might be hard-pressed to keep her laurels green, but Boston herself has no fears. Her present may not shine with so unique a brilliance as her past, but her past gains in luster with each succeeding year. Nothing can ever take from Boston her high literary prestige.

While we are still on Beacon Hill we can look out, not only upon the past, but upon the future. Those white domes and pillars gleaming like Greek temples across the blue Charles, are the new buildings of the Massachusetts Institute of Technology, and surely Greek temples were never lovelier, nor dedicated to more earnest pursuit of things not mundane. Quite as beautiful and quite as Grecian as the Technology buildings is the noble marble group of the School of Medicine of Harvard University, out by the Fenlands— that section of the city which is rapidly becoming a students' quarter, with its Simmons College, the New England Conservatory of Music, art schools, gymnasiums, private and technical schools of all descriptions, and its body of over 12,000 students. Harvard is, of course, across the river in Cambridge, and preparatory schools and colleges dot the suburbs in every direction, upholding the cultural traditions of a city which has proved itself peculiarly fitted to educational interests.

All this time we have, like *bona-fide* Bostonians, stayed on Beacon Hill, and merely looked out at the rest of the city. And perhaps this is as typical a thing as we could have done. Beacon Hill was the center of original Boston, when the Back Bay was merely a marsh, and long after the marsh was filled in and streets were laid out and handsome residences lined them, Beacon Hill looked down scornfully at the new section and murmured that it was built upon the discarded hoopskirts and umbrellas of the true Bostonians. Even when almost every one was crowded off the Hill and the Back Bay became the more aristocratic section of the two, there were still enough of the original inhabitants left to scorn these upstart social pretensions. And now Beacon Hill is again coming back into her own: the fine old houses are being carefully, almost worshipfully restored, probably never again to lose their rightful place in the general life of the city.

But if Beacon Hill was conservative in regard to the Back Bay, that district, in its turn, showed an equal unprogressiveness in regard to the Esplanade. To the stranger in Boston, delighting in that magnificent walk along the Charles River Embankment, with the arching spans of the Cambridge and Harvard bridges on one side, and the homes of wealth and mellow refinement on the other—a walk which for invigorating beauty compares with any in the cities of men—it seems incredible that when this promenade was laid out a few years ago, the householders along the water's edge absolutely refused to turn their front windows away from Beacon Street. Furthermore, they ignored the fact that their back yards and back windows presented an unbecoming face to such an incomparably lovely promenade, and the inevitable household rearrangement—by which the drawing-rooms were placed in the rear—was literally years in process of achievement. But such conservatism is one of Boston's idiosyncrasies, which we must accept like the wind and the flat A.

Present-day Bostonians are proud—and properly so—of their Copley Square, with its Public Library, rich with the mural paintings of Puvis de Chavannes, with Abbey's "Quest of the Holy Grail," and Sargent's "Frieze of the Prophets"; with its well-loved Trinity Church and with much excellent sculpture by Bela Pratt. Copley Square is the cultural center of modern Boston. The famous Lowell lectures—established about seventy-five years ago as free gifts to the people—are enthusiastically attended by audiences as Bostonese as one could hope to congregate; and in all sorts of queer nests in this vicinity are Theosophical reading-rooms, small halls where Buddhism is studied or New Thought taught, and half a hundred very new or very old philosophies, religions, fads, fashions, reforms, and isms find shelter. It is easy to linger in Copley Square: indeed, hundreds and hundreds of men and women—principally women—come from all over the United States for the sole purpose of spending a few months or a season in this very place, enjoying the lectures, concerts, and art exhibitions which are so easily and freely accessible. But in this bird's-eye flight across the historical and geographical map of a city that tempts one to many pleasant delays, we must hover for a brief moment over the South and the North Ends.

Skipping back, then, almost three centuries, but not traveling far as distance goes, the stranger in Boston cannot do better than to find his way from Copley Square to the Old South Church on Washington Street— that venerable building whose desecration by the British troops in 1775 the citizens found it so hard ever to forgive. It was here that Benjamin Franklin was baptized in 1706; here that Joseph Warren made a dramatic entry to the pulpit by way of the window in order to denounce the British soldiers; and here that momentous meetings were held in the heaving days before the Revolution. The Old South Church Burying Ground is now called the King's Chapel Burying Ground, and King's Chapel itself—a quaint, dusky building, suggestive of a London chapel—is only a few blocks away. Across its doorsill have not only stepped the Royal Governors of pre-Revolutionary days, but

Washington, General Gage, the indestructibly romantic figures of Sir Harry Frankland and Agnes Surriage; the funeral processions of General Warren and Charles Sumner. The organ, which came from England in 1756, is said to have been selected by Handel at the request of King George, and along the walls of the original King's Chapel were hung the escutcheons of the Kings of England and of the Royal Governors.

The Old State House is in this vicinity and is worthy—as are, indeed, both the Old South Church and King's Chapel—of careful architectural study and enjoyment. There are portraits, pictures, relics, and rooms within, and without the beautifully quaint lines and truly lovely details of the façade infuse a perpetual charm into the atmosphere of the city. It was directly in front of this building that the Boston Massacre took place in 1770, and from this second-story balcony that the repeal of the Stamp Act was read, and ten years later the full text of the Declaration of Independence.

Perhaps the next most interesting building in this section of old Boston is Faneuil Hall, the "Cradle of Liberty" whose dignified, old-fashioned proportions were not lost—thanks to Bulfinch—when it was enlarged. A gift of a public-spirited citizen, this building has served in a double capacity for a hundred and seventy-seven years, having public market-stalls below and a large hall above—a hall which is never rented, but used freely by the people whenever they wish to discuss public affairs. It would be impossible to enumerate the notable speakers and meetings which have rendered this hall famous, from General Gage down to Daniel Webster, Theodore Roosevelt, and Marshal Joffre.

If you are fond of water sights and smells you can step from Faneuil Hall down to a region permeated with the flavor of salt and the sound of shipping, a region of both ancient tradition and present activity. Here is India Wharf, its seven-story yellow-brick building once so tremendously significant of Boston's shipping prosperity; Long Wharf, so named because when it was built it was the longest in the country, and bore a battery at its end; Central Wharf, with its row of venerable stone warehouses; T Wharf, immensely picturesque with its congestion of craft of all descriptions; Commercial Wharf, where full-rigged sailing vessels which traded with China and India and the Cape of Good Hope were wont to anchor a hundred years ago. All this region is crammed with the paraphernalia of a typical water-front: curious little shops where sailors' supplies are sold; airy lofts where sails are cut and stitched and repaired; fish stores of all descriptions; sailors' haunts, awaiting the pen of an American Thomas Burke. The old Custom House where Hawthorne unwillingly plodded through his enforced routine is here, and near it the new Custom House rears its tower four hundred and ninety-eight feet above the sidewalk, a beacon from both land and sea.

The North End of Boston has not fared as well as the South End. The sons of Abraham and immigrants from Italy have appropriated the streets, dwellings, churches, and shops of the entire region, and even Christ Church (the famous Old North Church) has a Chiesa Italiana on its grounds. There are many touches to stir the memory in this Old North Church. The chime of eight bells naïvely stating, "We are the first ring of bells cast for the British Empire in North America"; the pew with the inscription that is set apart for the use of the "Gentlemen of Bay of Honduras"——visiting merchants who contributed the spire to the church in 1740; vaults beneath the church, forbidden now to visitors, where lie the bones of many Revolutionary heroes; a unique collection of vellum-covered books, and a few highly precious pieces of ancient furniture. The most conspicuous item about the church, of course, is that from its tower were hung the signal lanterns of Paul Revere, destined to shine imperishably down the ever-lengthening aisles of American history.

Before we press on to Bunker Hill—for that is our final destination— we should cast a glance at Copp's Hill Burying Ground, that hillside refuge where one can turn either back to the annals of the past or look out over the roof-tops and narrow streets to the present and the future. If you chose the latter, you can see easily Boston Harbor and Charlestown Navy Yard— that navy yard which has outstripped even its spectacular traditions by its stirring achievements in the Great War. "Old Ironsides" will lie here forever in the well-earned serenity of a secure old age, and it is probable that another visitor, the Kronprinzessin Cecilie, although lost under the name of the Mount Vernon and a coat of gray paint, will be long preserved in maritime memory.

The plain shaft of Bunker Hill Monument, standing to mark the spot where the Americans lost a battle that was, in reality, a victory, is like a blank mirror, reflecting only that which one presents to it. According to your historical knowledge and your emotional grasp Bunker Hill Monument is significant.

Skimming thus over the many-storied city, in a sort of literary airplane, it has been possible to point out only a few of the most conspicuous places and towers. The Common lies like a tiny pocket handkerchief of path-marked green at the foot of crowded Beacon Hill; the white Esplanade curves beside the blue Charles; the Back Bay is only a checkerboard of streets, alphabetically arranged; Copley Square is hardly distinguishable. The spires of the Old South Church, King's Chapel, the Old State House, and Faneuil Hall punctuate the South End; the North Church, the North End. The new Custom House Tower and Bunker Hill Monument seem hardly more than the minarets of a child's toy village.

The writer, as a pilot over this particular city, alights and resigns, commending for more detailed study, and for delightful guidance, Robert Shackleton's "Book of Boston." Let us now leave the city and set out in a more leisurely fashion on our way to Plymouth.

THE OLD COAST ROAD

From Boston to Plymouth

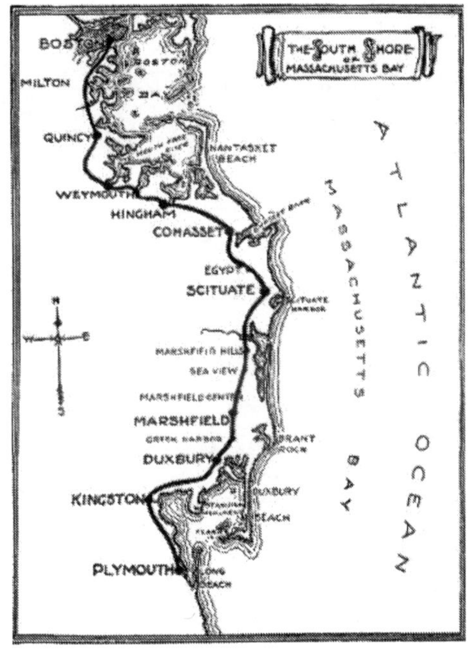

The South Shore of MASSACHUSETTS BAY

THE OLD COAST ROAD

CHAPTER I

DORCHESTER HEIGHTS AND THE OLD COAST ROAD

The very earliest of the great roads in New England was the Old Coast Road, connecting Boston with Plymouth—capitals of separate colonies. Do we, casually accepting the fruit of three hundred years of toil on this continent— do we, accustomed to smooth highways and swift and easy transportation, realize the significance of such a road?

A road is the symbol of the civilization which has produced it. The main passageway from the shore of the Yellow Sea to the capital of Korea, although it has been pressed for centuries immemorial by myriads of human feet, has never been more than a bridle path. On the other hand, wherever the great Roman Empire stepped, it engineered mighty thoroughfares which are a marvel to this day. A road is the thread on which the beads of history are strung; the beads of peace as well as those of war. Thrilling as is the progress of aerial navigation, with its infinite possibilities of human intercourse, yet surely, when the entire history of man is unrolled, the moment of the conception of building a wide and permanent road, instead of merely using a trail, will rank as equally dramatic. The first stone laid by the first Roman (they to whom the idea of road-building was original) will be recognized as significant as the quiver of the wings of the first airplane.

Let us follow the old road from Boston to Plymouth: follow it, not with undue exactitude, and rather too hastily, as is the modern way, but comfortably, as is also the modern way, picking up what bits of quaint lore and half-forgotten history we most easily may.

I think that as we start down this historic highway, we shall encounter—if our mood be the proper one in which to undertake such a journey—a curious procession coming down the years to meet us. We shall not call them ghosts, for they are not phantoms severed from earth, but, rather, the permanent possessors of the highway which they helped create.

We shall meet the Indian first, running lightly on straight, moccasined feet, along the trail from which he has burned, from time to time, the underbrush.

He does not go by land when he can go by water, but in this case there are both land and water to meet, for many are the streams, and they are unbridged as yet. With rhythmic lope, more beautiful than the stride of any civilized limbs, and with a sure divination of the best route, he chooses the trail which will ultimately be the highway of the vast army of pale-faces. Speed on, O solitary Indian—to vanish down the narrow trail of your treading as you are destined, in time, to vanish forever from the vision of New England!... Behind the red runner plod two stern-faced Pilgrims, pushing their way up from Plymouth toward the newer settlement at Massachusetts Bay. They come slowly and laboriously on foot, their guns cocked, eyes and ears alert, wading the streams without complaint or comment. They keep together, for no one is allowed to travel over this Old Coast Road single, "nor without some arms, though two or three together." The path they take follows almost exactly the trail of the Indian, seeking the fords, avoiding the morasses, clinging to the uplands, and skirting the rough, wooded heights.... After them—almost a decade after—we see a man on horseback, with his wife on a pillion behind him. They carry their own provisions and those for the beast, now and then dismounting to lead the horse over difficult ground, and now and then blazing a tree to help them in their return journey—mute testimony to the cruder senses of the white man to whom woodcraft never becomes instinctive. The fact that this couple possesses a horse presages great changes in New England. Ferries will be established; tolls levied, bridges thrown across the streams which now the horses swim, or cross by having their front feet in one canoe ferry and their hind feet in another—the canoes being lashed together. As yet we see no vehicle of any kind, except an occasional sedan chair. (The first one of these of which we have knowledge was presented to Governor Winthrop as a portion of a capture from a Spanish galleon.) However, these are not common. In 1631 Governor Endicott of Salem wrote that he could not get to Boston to visit Governor Winthrop as he was not well enough to wade the streams. The next year we read of Governor Winthrop surmounting the difficulty when he goes to visit Governor Bradford, by being carried on the backs of Indians across the fords. (It took him two days to make the journey.)

It is not strange that we see no wheeled vehicles. In 1672 there were only six stage-coaches in the whole of Great Britain, and they were the occasion of a pamphlet protesting that they encouraged too much travel! At this time Boston had one private coach. Although one swallow may not make a summer, one stage-coach marks the beginning of a new era. The age of walking and horseback riding approaches its end; gates and bars disappear, the crooked farm lanes are gradually straightened; and in come a motley procession of chaises, sulkies, and two-wheeled carts—two-wheeled carts, not four. There are sleds and sleighs for winter, but the four-wheeled wagon was little used in New England until the turn of the century. And then they were emphatically objected to because of the wear and tear on the roads! In 1669 Boston enacted that all carts "within yͤe necke of Boston shall be and goe without shod wheels." This provision is entirely comprehensible, when we remember that there was no idea of systematic road repair. No tax was imposed for keeping the roads in order, and at certain seasons of the year every able-bodied man labored on the highways, bringing his own oxen, cart, and tools.

But as the Old Coast Road, which was made a public highway in 1639, becomes a genuine turnpike—so chartered in 1803—the good old coaching days are ushered in with the sound of a horn, and handsome equipages with well-groomed, well-harnessed horses ply swiftly back and forth. Genial inns, with swinging pictorial signboards (for many a traveler cannot read), spring up along the way, and the post is installed.

But even with fair roads and regular coaching service, New England, separated by her fixed topographical outlines, remains provincial. It is not until the coming of the railroad, in the middle of the nineteenth century, that the hills are overcome, and she ceases to be an exclusively coastwise community and becomes an integral factor in the economic development of the whole United States.

Thus, then, from a thin thread of a trail barely wide enough for one moccasined foot to step before the other, to a broad, leveled thoroughfare, so wide that three or even four automobiles may ride abreast, and so clean that at the end of an all-day's journey one's face is hardly dusty, does the history of the Old Coast Road unroll itself. We who contemplate making the trip ensconced in the upholstered comfort of a machine rolling on air-filled tires, will, perhaps, be less petulant of some strip of roughened macadam, less bewildered by the characteristic windings, if we recall something of the first back-breaking cart that—not so very long ago—crashed over the stony road, and toilsomely worked its way from devious lane to lane.

Before we start down the Old Coast Road it may be enlightening to get a bird's-eye glimpse of it actually as we have historically, and for such a glimpse there is no better place than on the topmost balcony of the Soldier's Monument on Dorchester Heights. The trip to Dorchester Heights, in South Boston, is, through whatever environs one approaches it, far from attractive. This section of the city, endowed with extraordinary natural beauty and advantage of both land and water, and irrevocably and brilliantly graven upon the annals of American history, has been allowed to lose its ancient prestige and to sink low indeed in the social scale.

Nevertheless it is to Dorchester Heights that we, as travelers down the Old Coast Road, and as skimmers over the quickly turning pages of our early New England history, must go, and having once arrived at that lovely green eminence, whitely pointed with a marble shaft of quite unusual excellence, we must grieve once more that this truly glorious spot, with its unparalleled view far down the many-islanded harbor to the east and far over the famous city to the west, is not more frequented, more enjoyed, more honored.

If you find your way up the hill, into the monument, and up the stairs out to the balcony, probably you will encounter no other tourist. Only when you reach the top and emerge into the blue upper air you will meet those friendly winged visitors who frequent all spires——Saint Mark's in Venice or the Soldier's Monument in South Boston——the pigeons! Yes, the pigeons have discovered the charm of this lofty loveliness, and whenever the caretaker turns away his vigilant eye, they haste to build their nests on balcony or stair. They alone of Boston's residents enjoy to the full that of which too many Bostonians ignore the existence. Will you read the inscriptions first and recall the events which have raised this special hill to an historic eminence equal to its topographical one? Or will you look out first, on all sides and see the harbor, the city and country as it is to-day? Both surveys will be brief; perhaps we will begin with the latter.

Before us, to the wide east, lies Boston Harbor, decked with islands so various, so fascinating in contour and legend, that more than one volume has been written about them and not yet an adequate one. From the point of view of history these islands are pulsating with life. From Castle Island (on the left) which was selected as far back as 1634 to be a bulwark of the port, and which, with its Fort Independence, was where many of our Civil War soldiers received their training, to the outline of Squantum (on the right), where in October, 1917, there lay a marsh, and where, ten months later, the destroyer Delphy was launched from a shipyard that was a miracle of modern engineering—every mile of visible land is instinct with war-time associations.

But history is more than battles and forts and the paraphernalia of war; history is economic development as well. And from this same balcony we can pick out Thompson's, Rainsford, and Deer Island, set aside for huge corrective institutions——a graphic example of a nation's progress in its treatment of the wayward and the weak.

But if history is more than wars, it is also more than institutions. If it is the record of man's daily life, the pleasures he works for, then again we are standing in an unparalleled spot to look down upon its present-day manifestations. From City Point with its Aquarium, from the Marine Park with its long pleasure pier, to Nantasket with its flawless beach, this is the summer playground of unnumbered hosts. Boaters, bathers, picnickers—— all find their way here, where not only the cool breezes sweep their city-heated cheeks, but the forever bewitching passage of vessels in and out, furnishes endless entertainment. They know well, these laughing pleasure-seekers, crowding the piers and boats and wharves and beaches, where to come for refreshment, and now and then, in the history of the harbor, a solitary individual has taken advantage of the romantic charm which is the unique heritage of every island, and has built his home and lived, at least some portion of his days, upon one.

Apple Island, that most perfectly shaped little fleck of land of ten acres, was the home of a Mr. March, an Englishman who settled there with his family, and lived there happily until his death, being buried at last upon its western slope. The fine old elms which adorned it are gone now, as have the fine old associations. No one followed Mr. March's example, and Apple Island is now merely another excursion point.

On Calf Island, another ten-acre fragment, one of America's popular actresses, Julia Arthur, has her home. Thus, here and there, one stumbles upon individuals or small communities who have chosen to live out in the harbor. But one cannot help wondering how such beauty spots have escaped being more loved and lived upon by men and women who recognize the romantic lure which only an island can possess.

Of course the advantage of these positions has been utilized, if not for dwellings. Government buildings, warehouses, and the great sewage plant all find convenient foothold here. The excursionists have ferreted out whatever beaches and groves there may be. One need not regret that the harbor is not appreciated, but only that it has not been developed along æsthetic as well as useful lines.

We have been looking at the east, which is the harbor view. If we look to the west we see the city of Boston: the white tower of the Custom House; the gold dome of the State House; the sheds of the great South Station; the blue line of the Charles River. Here is the place to come if one would see a living map of the city and its environs. Standing here we realize how truly Boston is a maritime city, and standing here we also realize how it is that Dorchester Heights won its fame.

It was in the winter of 1776, when the British, under Lord Howe, were occupying Boston, and had fortified every place which seemed important. By some curious oversight—which seems incredible to us as we actually stand upon the top of this conspicuous hill—they forgot this spot.

When Washington saw what they had not seen—how this unique position commanded both the city and the harbor—he knew that his opportunity had come. He had no adequate cannon or siege guns, and the story of how Henry Knox—afterward General Knox—obtained these from Ticonderoga and brought them on, in the face of terrific difficulties of weather and terrain, is one that for bravery and brains will never fail to thrill. On the night of March 4, the Americans, keeping up a cannonading to throw the British off guard, and to cover up the sound of the moving, managed to get two thousand Continental troops and four hundred carts of fascines and intrenching tools up on the hill. That same night, with the aid of the moonlight, they threw up two redoubts—performing a task, which, as Lord Howe exclaimed in dismay the following morning, was "more in one night than my whole army could have done in a month."

The occupation of the heights was a magnificent *coup*. The moment the British saw what had been done, they realized that they had lost the fight. However, Lord Percy hurried to make an attack, but the weather made it impossible, and by the time the weather cleared the Americans were so strongly intrenched that it was futile to attack. Washington, although having been granted permission by Congress to attack Boston, wished to save the loyal city if possible. Therefore, he and Howe made an agreement by which Howe was to evacuate and Washington was to refrain from using his guns. After almost two weeks of preparation for departure, on March 17 the British fleet, as the gilded letters on the white marble panel tell us, in the words of Charles W. Eliot:

Carrying 11,000 effective men
And 1000 refugees
Dropped down to Nantasket Roads
And thenceforth
Boston was free
A strong British force
Had been expelled
From one of the United American colonies

The white marble panel, with its gold letters and the other inscriptions on the hill, tell the whole story to whoever cares to read, only omitting to mention that the thousand self-condemned Boston refugees who sailed away with the British fleet were bound for Halifax, and that that was the beginning of the opprobrious term: "Go to Halifax."

That the battle was won without bloodshed in no way minimizes the verdict of history that "no single event had a greater general effect on the course of the war than the expulsion of the British from the New England capital." And surely this same verdict justifies the perpetual distinction of this unique and beautiful hill.

This, then, is the story of Dorchester Heights—a story whose glory will wax rather than wane in the years, and centuries, to come. Let us be glad that out of the reek of the modern city congestion this green hill has been preserved and this white marble monument erected. Perhaps you see it now with different, more sympathetic eyes than when you first looked out from the balcony platform. Before us lies the water with its multifarious islands, bays, promontories, and coves, some of which we shall now explore. Behind us lies the city which we shall now leave. The Old Coast Road—the oldest in New England—winds from Boston to Plymouth, along yonder southern horizon. More history than one person can pleasantly relate, or one can comfortably listen to, lies packed along this ancient turnpike: incidents closer set than the tombs along the Appian Way. We will not try to hear them all. Neither will we follow the original road too closely, for we seek the beautiful pleasure drive of to-day more than the historic highway of long ago.

Boston was made the capital of the Massachusetts Bay Colony in 1632. Plymouth was a capital a decade before. It is to Plymouth that we now set out.

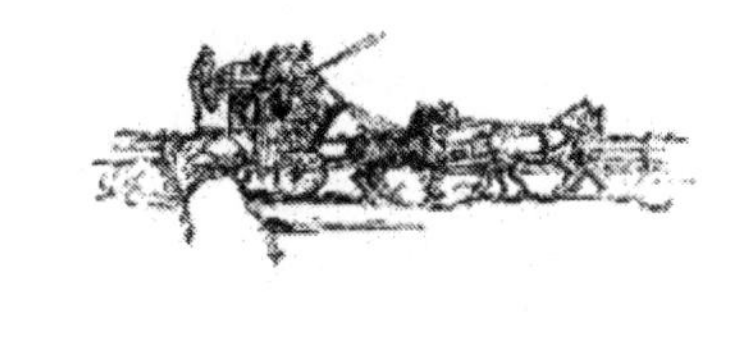

Chapter II

MILTON AND THE BLUE HILLS

Milton—a town of dignity and distinction! A town of enterprise and character! Ever since the first water-power mill in this country; the first powder mill in this country; the first chocolate mill in this country, and thus through a whole line of "first" things—the first violoncello, the first pianoforte, the first artificial spring leg, and the first railroad to see the light of day saw it in this grand old town—the name of Milton has been synonymous with initiative and men and women of character.

Few people to-day think of Milton in terms of industrial repute, but, rather, as a place of estates, too aristocratic to be fashionable, of historic houses, and of charming walks and drives and views. Many of the old families who have given the town its prestige still live in their ancestral manors, and many of the families who have moved there in recent years are of such sort as will heighten the fame of the famous town. As the stranger passes through Milton he is captivated by glimpses of ancient homesteads, settling behind their white Colonial fences topped with white Colonial urns, half hidden by their antique trees with an air of comfortable ease; of new houses, elegant and yet informal; of cottages with low roofs; of well-bred children playing on the wide, green lawns under the supervision of white-uniformed nurses; of old hedges, old walls, old trees; new roads, old drives, new gardens, and old gardens—everything well placed, well tended, everything presenting that indescribable atmosphere of well-established prosperity that scorns show; of breeding that neither parades nor conceals its quality. Yes—this is Milton; this is modern Milton. Boston society receives some of its most prominent contributions from this patrician source. But modern Milton is something more than this, as old Milton was something more than this.

For Milton, from this day of its birth, and countless centuries before its
birth as a town, has lived under the lofty domination of the Blue Hills, that
range of diaphanous and yet intense blue, that swims forever against the sky,
that marches forever around the horizon. The rounded summits of the Blue
Hills, to which the eye is irresistibly attracted before entering the town which
principally claims them, are the worn-down stumps of ancient mountains, and
although so leveled by the process of the ages, they are still the highest land
near the coast from Maine to Mexico. These eighteen or twenty skyey crests
form the southern boundary of the so-called Boston Basin, and are the most
prominent feature of the southern coast. From them the Massachuset tribe
about the Bay derived its name, signifying "Near the Great Hills," which
name was changed by the English to Massachusetts, and applied to both
bay and colony. Although its Indian name has been taken from this lovely
range, the loveliness remains. All the surrounding country shimmers under
the mysterious bloom of these heights, so vast that everything else is dwarfed
beside them, and yet so curiously airy that they seem to perpetually ripple
against the sky. The Great Blue Hill, especially—the one which bears an
observatory on its summit—swims above one's head. It seems to have a
singular way of moving from point to point as one motors, and although one
may be forced to admit that this may be due more to the winding roads than
to the illusiveness of the hill, still the buoyant effect is the same.

Ruskin declares somewhere, with his quaint and characteristic mixture
of positiveness and idealism, that "inhabitants of granite countries have a

force and healthiness of character about them that clearly distinguishes them from the inhabitants of less pure districts." Perhaps he was right, for surely here where the succeeding generations have all lived in the atmosphere of the marching Blue Hill, each has through its own fair name, done honor to the fair names which have preceded it.

One of the very first to be attracted by the lofty and yet lovely appeal of this region was Governor Thomas Hutchinson, the last of the Royal Governors Massachusetts was to know. It was about the middle of the eighteenth century that this gentleman, of whom John Adams wrote, "He had been admired, revered, and almost adored," chose as the spot for his house the height above the Neponset River. If we follow the old country Heigh Waye to the top of Unquity (now Milton) Hill, we will find the place he chose, although the house he built has gone and another stands in its place. Fairly near the road, it overlooked a rolling green meadow (a meadow which, by the gift of John Murray Forbes, will always be kept open), with a flat green marsh at its feet and the wide flat twist of the Neponset River winding through it, for all the world like a decorative panel by Puvis de Chavannes. One can see a bit of the North Shore and Boston Harbor from here. This is the view that the Governor so admired, and tradition tells us that when he was forced to return to England he walked on foot down the hill, shaking hands with his neighbors, patriot and Tory alike, with tears in his eyes as he left behind him the garden and the trees he had planted, and the house where he had so happily lived. Although the view from the front of the house is exquisite, the view from the back holds even more intimate attraction. Here is the old, old garden, and although the ephemeral blossoms of the present springtime shine brightly forth, the box, full twenty feet high, speaks of another epoch. Foxgloves lean against the "pleached alley," and roses clamber on a wall that doubtless bore the weight of their first progenitors.

Another governor who chose to live in Milton was Jonathan Belcher, but one fancies it was the grandness rather than the sweetness of the scene which attracted this rather spectacular person. The Belcher house still exists, as does the portrait of its master, in his wig and velvet coat and waistcoat, trimmed with richest gold lace at the neck and wrists. Small-clothes and gold knee and shoe buckles complete the picture of one who, when his mansion was planned, insisted upon an avenue fifty feet wide, and so nicely graded that visitors on entering from the street might see the gleam of his gold knee buckles as he stood on the distant porch. The avenue, however, was never completed, as Belcher was appointed governor of, and transferred to, New Jersey shortly after.

Two other men of note, who, since the days of our years are but threescore and ten, chose that their days without number should be spent in the town they loved, were Wendell Phillips and Rimmer the sculptor, who are both buried at Milton.

Not only notable personages, but notable events have been engendered under the shadow of these hills. The Suffolk Resolves, which were the prelude of the Declaration of Independence, were adopted at the Vose House, which still stands, square and unadorned, easy of access from the sidewalk, as is suitable for a home of democracy. The first piano ever made in this country received its conception and was brought to fulfillment in the Crehore house, which, although still sagging a bit, is by no means out of commission. And Wilde's Tavern, where was formed the public opinion in a day when the forming of public opinion was of preëminent importance, still retains, in its broad, hospitable lines, some shred of its ancient charm.

Milton is full of history. From the Revolutionary days, when the cannonading at Bunker Hill shook the foundations of the houses, but not the nerves of the Milton ladies, down to the year 1919, when the Fourth Liberty Loan of $2,955,250 was subscribed from a population of 9000, all the various vicissitudes of peace and war have been sustained on the high level that one might expect from men and women nobly nurtured by the strength of the hills.

How much of its success Milton attributes to its location—for one joins, indeed, a distinguished fellowship when one builds upon a hill, or on several hills, as Roman as well as Bostonian history testifies—can only be guessed by its tribute in the form of the Blue Hills Reservation. This State recreation park and forest reserve of about four thousand acres—a labyrinth of idyllic footpaths and leafy trails, of twisting drives and walks that open out upon superb vistas, is now the property of the people of Massachusetts. The granite quarry man—far more interested in the value of the stone that underlay the wooded slopes than in Ruskin's theory of its purifying effect upon the inhabitants—had already obtained a footing here, when, under the able leadership of Charles Francis Adams, the whole region was taken over by the State in 1894.

As you pass through the Reservation—and if you are taking even the most cursory glimpse of Milton you must include some portion of this park— you will pass the open space where in the early days, when Milton country life was modeled upon English country life more closely than now, Malcolm Forbes raced upon his private track the horses he himself had bred. The race-track with its judges' stands is still there, but there are no more horse-races, although the Forbes family still holds a conspicuous place in all the social as well as the philanthropic enterprises of the countryside. You may see, too, a solitary figure with a scientist's stoop, or a tutor with a group of boys, making a first-hand study of a region which is full of interest to the geologist.

Circling thus around the base of the Great Blue Hill and irresistibly drawn closer and closer to it as by a magnet, one is impelled to make the ascent to the top—an easy ascent with its destination clearly marked by the Rotch Meteorological Observatory erected in 1884 by the late A. Lawrence Rotch of Milton, who bequeathed funds for its maintenance. It is now connected with Harvard University.

Once at the top the eye is overwhelmed by a circuit of more than a hundred and fifty miles! It is almost too immense at first—almost as barren as an empty expanse of rolling green sea. But as the eye grows accustomed to the stretching distances, objects both near and far begin to appear. And soon, if the day is clear, buildings may be identified in more than one hundred and twenty-five villages. We are six hundred and thirty-five feet above the sea, on the highest coastland from Agamenticus, near York, Maine, to the Rio Grande, and the panorama thus unrolled is truly magnificent. Facing northerly we can easily distinguish Cambridge, Somerville, and Malden, and far beyond the hills of Andover and Georgetown. A little to the east, Boston with its gilded dome; then the harbor with its islands, headlands, and fortifications. Beyond that are distinctly visible various points on the North Shore, as far as Eastern Point Lighthouse in Gloucester. Forty miles to the northeast appear the twin lighthouses on Thatcher's Island, seeming, from here, to be standing, not on the land, but out in the ocean. Nearer and more distinct is Boston Light—a sentinel at the entrance to the harbor, while beyond it stretches Massachusetts Bay. Turning nearly east the eye, passing over Chickatawbut Hill—three miles off and second in height of the Blue Hills—follows the beautiful curve of Nantasket Beach, and the pointing finger of Minot's Light. Facing nearly south, the long ridge of Manomet Hill in Plymouth, thirty-three miles away, stands clear against the sky, while twenty-six miles away, in Duxbury, one sees the Myles Standish Monument. Directly south rises the smoke of the city of Fall River; to the westerly, Woonsocket, and continuing to the west, Mount Wachusett in Princeton. Far to the right of Wachusett, nearly over the dome of the Dedham Courthouse, rounds up Watatic in Ashburnham, and northwest a dozen peaks of southern New Hampshire. At the right of Watatic and far beyond it is the Grand Monadnock in Jaffrey, 3170 feet above the sea and sixty-seven and a half miles away. On the right of Grand Monadnock is a group of nearer summits: Mount Kidder, exactly northwest; Spofford and Temple Mountains; then appears the remarkable Pack-Monadnock, near Peterboro, with its two equal summits. The next group to the right is in Lyndeboro. At the right of Lyndeboro, and nearly over the Readville railroad stations, is Joe English Hill, and to complete the round, nearly north-northwest are the summits of the Uncanoonuc Mountains, fifty-nine miles away.

This, then, is the Great Blue Hill of Milton. Those who are familiar with the State of Massachusetts—and New England—can stand here and pick out a hundred distinguishing landmarks, and those who have never been here before may find an unparalleled opportunity to see the whole region at one sweep of the eye.

From the point of view of topography the summit of Great Blue Hill is the place to reach. But for the sense of mysterious beauty, for snatches of pictures one will never forget, the little vistas which open on the upward or the downward trail, framed by hanging boughs or encircled by a half frame of stone and hillside—these are, perhaps, more lovely. The hill itself, seen from a distance, floating lightly like a vast blue ball against a vaster sky, is dreamily suggestive in a way which the actual view, superb as it is, is not. One remembers Stevenson's observation, that sometimes to travel hopefully is better than to arrive. So let us come down, for, after all, "Love is of the valley." Down again to the old town of Milton. We have not half begun to wander over it: not half begun to hear the pleasant stories it has to tell. When one is as old as this—for Milton was discovered by a band from Plymouth who came up the Neponset River in 1621—one has many tales to tell.

Of all the towns along the South Shore there are few whose feet are so firmly emplanted in the economic history of the past and present as is Milton. That peculiar odor of sweetness which drifts to us with a turn of the wind, comes from a chocolate mill whose trade-mark of a neat-handed maid with her little tray is known all over the civilized world. And those mills stand upon the site of the first grist mill in New England to be run by water power. This was in 1634, and one likes to picture the sturdy colonists trailing into town, their packs upon their backs, like children in kindergarten games, to have their grain ground. Israel Stoughton was the name of the man who established this first mill—a name perpetuated in the near-by town of Stoughton.

All ground is historic ground in Milton. That rollicking group of schoolboys yonder belongs to an academy, which, handsome and flourishing as it is to-day, was founded as long ago as 1787. That seems long ago, but there was a school in Milton before that: a school held in the first meeting-house. Nothing is left of this quaint structure but a small bronze bas-relief, set against a stone wall, near its original site. This early church and early school was a log cabin with a thatched roof and latticed windows, if one may believe the relief, but men of brains and character were taught there lessons which stood them and the colony in good stead. One fancies the students' roving eyes may have occasionally strayed down the Indian trail directly opposite the old site—a trail which, although now attained to the proud rank of a lane, Churchill's Lane, still invites one down its tangled green way along the gray stone wall. Yes, every step of ground has its tradition here. Yonder railroad track marks the spot where the very first tie in the country was laid, and laid for no less significant purpose than to facilitate the carrying of granite blocks for Bunker Hill Monument from their quarry to the harbor.

Granite from the hills—the hills which swim forever against the sky and march forever above the distant horizon. Again we are drawn back to the irresistible magnet of those mighty monitors. Yes, wherever one goes in Milton, either on foot to-day or back through the chapters of three centuries ago, the Blue Hills dominate every event, and the Great Blue Hill floats above them all.

"I will lift up mine eyes unto the hills from whence cometh my help," chants the psalmist. Ah, well, no one can say it better than that—except the hills themselves, which, with gentle majesty, look down affectionately upon the town at their feet.

CHAPTER III

SHIPBUILDING AT QUINCY

The first man-made craft which floated on the waters of what is now Fore River was probably a little dugout, a crude boat made by an Indian, who burned out the center of a pine log which he had felled by girdling with fire. After he had burned out as much as he could, he scraped out the rest with a stone tool called a "celt." The whole operation probably took one Indian three weeks. The Rivadavia which slid down the ways of the Fore River Shipbuilding Corporation in August, 1914, weighed 13,400 tons and had engaged the labor of 2000 men for fifty months.

Between these two extremes flutter all the great sisterhood of shallops, sloops, pinks, schooners, snows, the almost obsolete batteau and periagua, the gundelow with its picturesque lateen sail, and all the winged host that are now merely names in New England's maritime history.

We may not give in this limited space an account of the various vessels which have sailed down the green-sea aisles the last three hundred years. But of the very first, "a great and strong shallop" built by the Plymouth settlers for fishing, we must make brief mention, and of the Blessing of the Bay, the first seaworthy native craft to be built and launched on these shores—the pioneer of all New England commerce. Built by Governor Winthrop, he notes of her in his journal on August 31, 1631, that "the bark being of thirty tons went to sea." That is all he says, but from that significant moment the building of ships went on "gallantly," as was indeed to be expected in a country whose chief industry was fishing and which was so admirably surrounded by natural bays and harbors. In 1665 we hear of the Great and General Court of Massachusetts—which distinctive term is still applied to the Massachusetts Legislature—forbidding the cutting of any trees suitable for masts. The broad arrow of the King was marked on all white pines, twenty-four inches in diameter, three feet from the ground. Big ships and little ships swarmed into existence, and every South Shore town made shipbuilding history. The ketch, a two-masted vessel carrying from fifteen to twenty tons, carried on most of the coasting traffic, and occasionally ventured on a foreign voyage. When we recall that the best and cheapest ships of the latter half of the seventeenth century were built here in the new country, we realize that shipyards, ports, docks, proper laws and regulations, and the invigorating progress which marks any thriving industry flourished bravely up and down the whole New England coast.

It is rather inspiring to stand here on the bridge which spans the Fore River, and picture that first crude dugout being paddled along by the steady stroke of the red man, and then to look at the river to-day. Every traveler through Quincy is familiar with the aerial network of steel scaffolding criss-crossing the sky, with the roofs of shops and offices and glimpses of vessels visible along the water-front. But few travelers realize that these are merely the superficial features of a shipyard which under the urge of the Great War delivered to the Navy, in 1918, eighteen completed destroyers, which was as many as all the other yards in the country put together delivered during this time. A shipyard which cut the time of building destroyers from anywhere between eighteen and thirty-two months to an average of six months and a half; a shipyard which made the world's record of one hundred and seventy-four days from the laying of the keel to the delivering of a destroyer.

It is difficult to grasp the meaning of these figures. Difficult, even after one has obtained entrance into this city within a city, and seen with his own eyes twenty thousand men toiling like Trojans. Seen a riveting crew which can drive more than twenty-eight hundred rivets in nine hours; battleships that weigh thirty thousand tons; a plate yard piled with steel plates and steel bars worth two million dollars; cranes that can lift from five tons up to others of one hundred tons capacity; single buildings a thousand feet long and eighty feet high.

Perhaps the enormousness of the plant is best comprehended, not when we mechanically repeat that it covers eighty acres and comprises eighty buildings, and that four full-sized steam locomotives run up and down its yard, but when we see how many of the intimate things of daily living have sprung up here as little trees spring up between huge stones. For the Fore River Plant is more than an industrial organization. It is a social center, an economic entity. It has its band and glee club, ball team and monthly magazine. There are refreshment stands, and a bathing cove; a brand-new village of four hundred and thirty-eight brand-new houses; dormitories which accommodate nearly a thousand men and possess every convenience and even luxuries. The men work hard here, but they are well paid for their work, as the many motor-cycles and automobiles waiting for them at night testify. It is a scene of incredible industry, but also of incredible completeness.

To look down upon the village and the yard from the throbbing roof of the steel mill, seven hundred and seventy feet long and a hundred and eighty-eight wide, is a thrilling sight. Within the yard, confined on three sides by its high fences and buildings and on the fourth by Weymouth Fore River, one sees, far below, locomotives moving up and down on their tracks; great cranes stalking long-leggedly back and forth; smoke from foundry, blacksmith shop, and boiler shop; men hurrying to and fro. Whistles blow, and whole buildings tremble. The smoke and the grayness might make it a gloomy scene if it were not for the red sides of the immense submarines gleaming in their wide slips to the water. Everywhere one sees the long gray sides of freighters, destroyers, merchant ships, and oil tankers heaving like the mailed ribs of sea animals basking on the shore. Practically every single operation, from the most stupendous to the most delicate, necessary for the complete construction of these vessels, is carried on in this yard. The eighty acres look small when we realize the extent and variety of the work achieved within its limits.

Yes, the solitary Indian, working with fire and celt on his dugout, would not recognize this once familiar haunt, nor would he know the purpose of these vast vessels without sail or paddle. And yet, were this same Indian standing on the roof with us, he would see a wide stream of water he knew well, and he would see, too, above the smoke of the furnace, shop, and boiler room, the friendly green of the trees.

Perhaps there is nothing which makes us realize the magical rapidity of growth so much as to look from this steel city and to see the woods close by. For instead of being surrounded by the sordid congestion of an industrial center, the Fore River Shipyard is in the midst of practically open country.

While we are speaking of rapidity we must look over toward the Victory Plant at Squantum, that miraculous marsh which was drained with such expedition that just twelve months from the day ground was broken for its foundation, it launched its first ship, and less than two years after completed its entire contract. Surely never in the history of shipbuilding have brain and brawn worked so brilliantly together!

In this way, then, the history of the ships that have sailed the seven seas has been built up at Quincy—a dramatic history and one instinct with the beauty which is part of gliding canoe and white sails, and part, too, of the huge smooth-slipping monsters of a modern day, sleek and swift as leviathans. But all the while the building of these ships has been going on, there has been slowly rising within the selfsame radius another ship, vaster, more inspiring, calling forth initiative even more intense, idealism even more profound—the Ship of State.

We who journey to-day over the smooth or troubled waters of national or international affairs are no more conscious of the infinite toil and labors which have gone into the intricate making of the vessel that carries us, than are travelers conscious of the cogs and screws, the engines and all the elaboration of detail which compose an ocean liner. Like them we sometimes grumble at meals or prices, at some discourtesy or incompetence, but we take it for granted that the engine is in commission, that the bottom is whole and the chart correct. The great Ship of State of this country may occasionally run into rough weather, but Americans believe that, in the last analysis, she is honestly built. And it is to Quincy that we owe a large initial part of this building.

It is astonishing to enumerate the notable public men, who have been influential in establishing our national policy, who have come from Quincy. There is no town in this entire country which can equal the record. What other town ever produced two Presidents of the United States, an Ambassador to Great Britain, a Governor of the Commonwealth, a Mayor of Boston, two presidents of Harvard University, and judges, chief justices, statesmen, and orators in such quantity and of such quality? Truly this group of eminent men of brilliance, integrity, and public feeling is unique in our history. To read the biographies of Quincy's great men would comprise a studious winter's employment, but we, passing through the historic city, may hold up our fragment of a mirror and catch a bit of the procession.

First and foremost, of course, will come President John Adams, he who, both before and after his term of high office, toiled terrifically in the public cause, being at the time of his election to Congress a member of ninety committees and a chairman of twenty-five! We see him as the portraits have taught us to see him, with strong, serious face,—austere, but not harsh,—velvet coat, white ruffles, and white curls. He stands before us as the undisputed founder of what is now recognized as American diplomacy. Straightforward, sound to the core, unswerving, veracious, exemplifying in every act the candor of the Puritan, so congruous with the new simple life of a nation of common people. I think we shall like best to study him as he stands at the door of the little house in which he was born, and which, with its pitch roof, its antique door and eaves, is still preserved, close to the street, for public scrutiny.

Next to President John Adams comes his son, John Quincy Adams, also a President of the United States. Spending much of his time abroad, the experience of those diplomatic years is graven upon features more subtly refined than those of his sire. But for all his foreign residence, he was, like his father, a Puritan in its most exalted sense; like him toiled all his life in public service, dying in the harness when rising to address the Speaker of the House. Him, too, we see best, standing at the door of his birthplace, a small cottage a stone's throw from the other cottage, separated only by a turnstile. Fresh white curtains hang in the small-paned windows; the grass is neatly trimmed, and like its quaint companion it is now open to the public and worth the tourist's call. Both these venerable cottages have inner walls, one of burnt, the other of unburnt brick; and both are unusual in having no boards on the outer walls, but merely clapboards fastened directly on to the studding with wrought-iron nails.

Still another Adams follows, Charles Francis Adams. Although a little boy when he first comes into public view, a little boy occupying the conspicuous place as child of one President and grandchild of another, yet he was to win renown and honor on his own account as Ambassador to England during the critical period of our Civil War. America remembers him best in this position. His firm old face with its white chin whiskers is a worthy portrait in the ancestral gallery.

Although the political history of this country may conclude its reference to the Adamses with these three famous figures, yet all New Englanders and all readers of biography would be reluctant to turn from this remarkable family without mention of the sons of Charles Francis Adams, two of whom have written, beside valuable historical works, autobiographies so entertaining and so truly valuable for their contemporaneous portraits as to win a place of survival in our permanent literature.

A member of the Adams family still lives in the comfortable home where the three first and most famous members all celebrated their golden weddings. This broad-fronted and hospitable house, built in 1730 by Leonard Vassal, a West India planter, for his summer residence, with its library finished in panels of solid mahogany, was confiscated when its Royalist owner fled at the outbreak of the Revolution, and John Adams acquired the property and left the pitch-roofed cottage down the street. The home of two Presidents, what tales it could tell of notable gatherings! One must read the autobiography of Charles Francis Adams and "The Education of Henry Adams" to appreciate the charm of the succeeding mistresses of the noble homestead, and to enjoy in retrospect its many illustrious visitors.

To have produced one family like the Adamses would surely be sufficient distinction for any one place, but the Adams family forms merely one unit in Quincy's unique procession of great men.

The Quincy family, for which the town was named, and which at an early date intermarried with the Adamses, presents an almost parallel distinction. The first Colonel Quincy, he who lived like an English squire, a trifle irascible, to be sure, but a dignified and commanding figure withal, had fourteen children by his first wife and three by his second, so the family started off with the advantage of numbers as well as of blood. At the Quincy mansion house were born statesmen, judges, and captains of war. The "Dorothy Q." of Holmes's poem first saw the light in it, and the Dorothy who became the bride of the dashing John Hancock blossomed into womanhood in it. Here were entertained times without number Sir Harry Vane, quaint Judge Sewall, Benjamin Franklin, and that couple who gleam through the annals of New England history in a never-fading flame of romance, Sir Harry Frankland and beautiful Agnes Surriage. The Quincy mansion, which was built about 1635 by William Coddington of Boston and occupied by him until he was exiled for his religious opinions, was bought by Edmund Quincy. His grandson, who bore his name, enlarged the house, and lived in it until his death when it descended to his son Edmund, the eminent jurist and father of Dorothy. The old-fashioned furniture, utensils and pictures, the broad hall, fine old stairway with carved balustrades, and foreign wall-paper supposed to have been hung in honor of the approaching marriage of Dorothy to John Hancock, are still preserved in their original place. Of the Quincy family, whose sedate jest it was that the estate descended from 'Siah to 'Siah, so frequent was the name "Josiah," the best known is perhaps the Josiah Quincy who was Mayor of Boston for six years and president of Harvard for sixteen. The portrait of his long, thin face is part of every New England history, and his busy, serene life, "compacted of Roman and Puritan virtues," is still upheld to all American children as a model of high citizenship.

But not even the long line of the Quincy family completes the list of the town's great men. Henry Hope, one of the most brilliant financiers of his generation, and founder of a European banking house second only to that of the Rothchilds, was a native of Quincy. John Hull—who, as every school-child knows, on the day of his daughter's marriage to Judge Sewall, placed her in one of his weighing scales, and heaped enough new pine-tree shillings into the other to balance, and then presented both to the bridegroom—held the first grant of land in the present town of Braintree (which originally included Quincy, Randolph, and Holbrook).

From the picturesque union of John Hull's bouncing daughter Betsy and Judge Sewall sprang the extraordinary family of Sewalls which has given three chief justices to Massachusetts, and one to Canada, and has been distinguished in every generation for the talents and virtues of its members. In passing, we may note that it was this same John Hull who named Point Judith for his wife, little dreaming what a *bête noir* the place would prove to mariners in the years to come.

There is another Quincy man whom it is pleasant to recall, and that is Henry Flynt, a whimsical and scholarly old bachelor, who was a tutor at Harvard for no less than fifty-three years, the one fixed element in the flow of fourteen college generations. One of the most accomplished scholars of his day, his influence on the young men with whom he came in contact was stimulating to a degree, and they loved to repeat bits of his famous repartee. A favorite which has come down to us was on an occasion when Whitefield the revivalist declared in a theological discussion: "It is my opinion that Dr. Tillotson is now in hell for his heresy." To which Tutor Flynt retorted dryly: "It is my opinion that you will not meet him there."

The procession of Quincy's great men which we have been watching winds its way, as human processions are apt to do, to the old graveyard. Most of the original settlers are buried here, although not a few were buried on their own land, according to the common custom. Probably this ancient burying ground, with its oldest headstone of 1663, has never been particularly attractive. The Puritans did not decorate their graveyards in any way. Fearing that prayers or sermons would encourage the "superstitions" of the Roman Catholic Church, they shunned any ritual over the dead or beautifying of their last resting-place. However, neglected as the spot was, the old stone church, whose golden belfry is such a familiar and pleasant landmark to all the neighboring countryside, still keeps its face turned steadfastly toward it. The congested traffic of the city square presses about its portico, but those who knew and loved it best lie quietly within the shadow of its gray walls. Under the portico lies President John Adams, and "at his side sleeps until the trump shall sound, Abigail, his beloved and only wife." In the second chamber is placed the dust of his illustrious son, with "His partner for fifty years, Louisa Catherine"——she of whom Henry Adams wrote, "her refined figure; her gentle voice and manner; her vague effect of not belonging there, but to Washington or Europe, like her furniture and writing-desk with little glass doors above and little eighteenth-century volumes in old binding."

It has been called the "church of statesmen," this dignified building, and so, indeed, might Quincy itself be called the "city of statesmen." It would be extremely interesting to study the reasons for Quincy's peculiar productiveness of noble public characters. The town was settled (as Braintree) exclusively by people from Devonshire and Lincolnshire and Essex. The laws of the Massachusetts Colony forbade Irish immigration——probably more for religious than racial reasons. On reading the ancient petition for the incorporation of the town one is struck by the fact that practically every single name of the one hundred and fifty signers is English in origin, the few which were not having been anglicized. All of these facts point to a homogeneous stock, with the same language, traditions, and social customs. Obviously there is a connection between the governmental genius displayed by Quincy's sons and the singular purity of the original English stock.

Little did Wampatuck, the son of Chickatawbut, realize what he was doing when he parted with his Braintree lands for twenty-one pounds and ten shillings. The Indian deed is still preserved, with the following words on its back: "In the 17th reign of Charles 2. Braintry Indian Deeds. Given 1665. Aug. 10: Take great care of it."

Little did the Indian chief realize that the surrounding waters were to float hulks as mighty as a city; that the hills were to furnish granite for buildings and monuments without number; and that men were to be born there who would shape the greatest Ship of State the world has ever known. And yet, if he had known, possibly he would have accepted the twenty-one pounds and ten shillings just the same, and departed quietly. For the ships that were to be built would never have pleased him as well as his own canoe; the granite buildings would have stifled him; and the zealous Adamses and the high-minded Quincys and Sewalls and all the rest would have bored him horribly. Probably the only item in the whole history of Quincy which would have appealed to Wampatuck in the least would have been the floating down on a raft of the old Hollis Street Church of Boston, to become the Union Church of Weymouth and Braintree in 1810. This and the similar transportation of the Bowditch house from Beacon Street in Boston to Quincy a couple of years later would have fascinated the red man, as the recital of the feat fascinates us to-day.

Those who care to learn more of Quincy will do well to read the autobiography of Charles Francis Adams and "The Education of Henry

Adams." Those who care more for places than for descriptions of them may wander at will, finding beneath the surface of the modern city many landmarks of the old city which underlies it. They may see the scaffolding of the great shipyards latticing themselves against the sky, and the granite quarries against the hills. They may see the little cottages and the great houses made famous by those who have passed over their thresholds; they may linger in the old burial ground and trace out the epitaphs under the portico of the golden-belfried church. But after they have touched and handled all of these things, they will not understand Quincy unless they look beyond and recognize her greatest contribution to this country—the noble statesmen who so bravely and intelligently toiled to construct America's Ship of State.

CHAPTER IV

THE ROMANCE OF WEYMOUTH

The paintings of John Constable, idyllic in their quietness, dewy in their serenity——how many travelers, how many lovers of art, superficial or profound, yearly seek out these paintings in the South Kensington Museum or the Louvre, and stand before them wrapt in gentle ecstasy?

The quality of Constable's pictures delineates in luminous softness a peculiarly lovely side of English rural life, but one need not travel to England or France to see this loveliness. Weymouth, that rambling stretch of towns and hamlets, of summer colony and suburb, possesses in certain areas bits of rural landscape as serene, as dewy, as idyllically tranquil as Constable at his best.

Comparatively few people in New England, or out of it, know Weymouth well. Every one has heard of it, for it is next in age to the town of Plymouth itself, and every one who travels to the South Shore passes some section of it, for it extends lengthily——north and south, east and west——being the only town in Massachusetts to retain its original boundaries. And numbers of people are familiar with certain parts of it, for there are half a score of villages in the township, some of them summer settlements, some of them animated by an all-the-year-round life. But compared with the other towns along this historic route, Weymouth as a whole is little known and little appreciated. And yet the history of Weymouth is not without amusing and edifying elements, and the scenery of Weymouth is worthy of the détour that strangers rarely make.

"Old Spain" is the romantic name for an uninteresting part of the township, and, conversely, Commercial Street is the uninteresting name for a romantic part. It is along a highway stigmatized by such a name that one gets the glimpses of a Constable country: glimpses of rolling meadows, of fertile groves, of cattle grazing in elm-shaded pastures, of a road winding contentedly among simple, ancient cottages, and quiet, thrifty farms. These are the homes which belong, and have belonged for generations, to people who are neither rich nor poor; cozy, quaint, suggesting in an odd way the thatched-roof cottages of England. Not that all of Weymouth's homes are of this order. The Asa Webb Cowing house, which terminates Commercial Street within a stone's throw of the square of the town of Weymouth, is one of the very finest examples of the Colonial architecture in this country. The exquisite tracery and carving over and above the front door, and the white imported marble window lintels spin an elaborate and marvelously fine lacework of white over the handsome red-brick façade. Although it is, alas, falling somewhat into disrepair, perfect proportion and gemlike workmanship still stamp the venerable mansion as one of patrician heritage. There are other excellent examples of architecture in Weymouth, but the Cowing house must always be the star, both because of its extraordinary beauty and conspicuous position. Yes, if you want a characteristic glimpse of Weymouth, you cannot do better than to begin in front of this landmark, and drive down Commercial Street. Here for several smiling miles there is nothing—no ugly building large or small, no ruthless invasion of modernity to mar the mood of happy simplicity. Her beauty of beach, of sky, of river, Weymouth shares with other South Shore towns. Her perfection of idyllic rusticity is hers alone.

Just as Weymouth's scenery is unlike that of her neighbors, so her history projects itself from an entirely different angle from theirs. While they were conceived by zealous, God-fearing men and women honestly seeking to establish homes in a new country, Weymouth was inadvertently born through the misconduct of a set of adventurers. Not every one who came to America in those significant early years came impelled by lofty motives. There were scapegraces, bad boys, rogues, mercenaries, and schemers; and perhaps it is entirely logical that the winning natural loveliness of this place should have lured to her men who were not of the caliber to face more exposed, less fertile sections, and men to whom beauty made an especial appeal.

The Indians early found Wessagusset, as they called it, an important rendezvous, as it was accessible by land and sea, and there were probably temporary camps there previous to 1620, formed by fishermen and traders who visited the New England coast to traffic with the natives. But it was not until the arrival of Thomas Weston in 1622 that Weymouth's history really begins. And then it begins in a topsy-turvy way, so unlike Puritan New England that it makes us rub our eyes, wondering if it is really true.

This Thomas Weston, who was a merchant adventurer of London, took it into his head to establish a colony in the new country entirely different from the Plymouth Colony. He had been an agent of the Pilgrims in their negotiations with the Plymouth Company, and when he broke off the connection it was to start a settlement which should combine all of the advantages, with none of the disadvantages, of the Plymouth Colony. First of all, it was to be a trading community pure and simple, with its object frankly to make money. Second, it was to be composed of men without families and familiar with hardship. And third, there was no religious motive or bond. That such an unidealistic enterprise should not flourish on American soil is worth noting. The disorderly, thriftless rabble, picked up from the London streets, soon got into trouble with the Indians and with neighboring colonists, and finally, undone by the results of their own improvidence and misbehavior, wailed that they "wanted to go back to London," to which end the Plymouth settlers willingly aided them, glad to get them out of the country. Thus ended the first inauspicious settlement of Weymouth.

The second, which was undertaken shortly after by Robert Gorges, broke up the following spring, leaving only a few remnants behind. Sir Ferdinando Gorges, who was not a Spaniard as his name suggests, but a picturesque Elizabethan and a kinsman of Sir Walter Raleigh, essayed (through his son Robert) an experimental government along practically the same commercial lines as had Weston, and his failure was as speedy and complete as Weston's had been.

A third attempt, while hardly more successful, furnishes one of the gayest and prettiest episodes in the whole history of New England. Across the somber procession of earnest-faced men and women, across the psalm-singing and the praying, across the incredible toil of the pioneers at Plymouth now flashes the brightly costumed and pleasure-loving courtier, Thomas Morton. An agent of Gorges, Morton with thirty followers floated into Wessagusset to found a Royalist and Episcopalian settlement. This Episcopalian bias was quite enough to account for Bradford's disparaging description of him as a "kind of petie-fogie of Furnifells Inn," and explains why the early historians never made any fuller or more favorable record than absolutely necessary of these neighbors of theirs, although the churchman Samuel Maverick admits that Morton was a "gentleman of good qualitee."

But it was for worse sins than his connection with the Established Church that Morton's name became synonymous with scandal throughout the whole Colony. In the very midst of the dun-colored atmosphere of Puritanism, in the very heart of the pious pioneer settlement this audacious scamp set up, according to Bradford, "a schoole of atheisme, and his men did quaff strong waters and comport themselves as if they had anew revived and celebrated the feasts of yͤe Roman Goddess Flora, or the beastly practises of yͤe madd Bachanalians." The charge of atheism in this case seems based on the fact that Morton used the Book of Common Prayer, but as for the rest, there is no question that this band of silken merry-makers imported many of the carnival customs and hereditary pastimes of Old England to the stern young New England; that they fraternized with the Indians, shared their strong waters with them, and taught them the use of firearms; and that Merrymount became indeed a scene of wildest revelry.

The site of Merrymount had originally been selected by Captain Wollaston for a trading post. Imbued with the same mercenary motive which had proved fatal in the case of Weston and Gorges, Captain Wollaston, whose name is perpetuated in Mount Wollaston, brought with him in 1625 a gang of indented white servants. Finding his system of industry ill suited to the climate, he carried his men to Virginia, where he sold them. When he left,

Morton took possession of the place and dubbed it "Ma-re-mount." And then began the pranks which shook the Colony to its foundations. Picture to yourself a band of sworn triflers, dedicated to the wildest philosophy of pleasure, teaching bears to dance, playing blind-man's buff, holding juggling and boxing matches, and dancing. According to Hawthorne, on the eve of Saint John they felled whole acres of forests to make bonfires, and crowned themselves with flowers and threw the blossoms into the flames. At harvest-time they hilariously wasted their scanty store of Indian corn by making an image with the sheaves, and wreathing it with the painted garlands of autumn foliage. They crowned the King of Christmas and bent the knee to the Lord of Misrule! Such fantastic foolery is inconceivable in a Puritan community, and the Maypole which was its emblem was the most inconceivable of all. This "flower-decked abomination," ornamented with white birch bark, banners, and blossoms, was the center of the tipsy jollity of Merrymount. As Morton explains: "A goodly pine tree of eighty foote was reared up, with a peare of bucks horns nayled on somewhere near to the top of it: where it stood as a faire sea mark for directions how to find out the way to mine host of Ma-re-mount." Around this famous, or infamous, pole Morton and his band frolicked with the Indians on May Day in 1627. As the indignant historian writes: "Unleashed pagans from the purlieus of the gross court of King James, danced about the Idoll of Merry Mount, joining hands with the lasses in beaver coats, and singing their ribald songs."

It doesn't look quite so heinous to us, this Maypole dancing, as it did to the outraged Puritans. In fact, the story of Morton and Merrymount is one of the few glistening threads in the somber weaving of those early days. But the New England soil was not prepared at that time to support any such exotic, and Myles Standish was sent to disperse the frivolous band, and to order Morton back to England, which he did, after a scrimmage which Morton relates with great vivacity and doubtful veracity in his "New English Canaan."

This "New English Canaan," by the way, had a rather singular career. Morton tells in it many amusing stories, and one of them was destined to a remarkable perpetuity in English literature. The story deals with the Wessagusset settlers promising to hang one of their own members who had been caught stealing—this hanging in order to appease the Indians. Morton gravely states that instead of hanging the real culprit, who was young and lusty, they hanged, in his place, another, old and sick. In his quaint diction: "You all agree that one must die, and one shall die, this young man's cloathes we will take off and put upon one that is old and impotent, a sickly person that cannot escape death, such is the disease on him confirmed, that die hee must. Put the young man's cloathes on this man, and let the sick person be hanged in the other's steade. Amen sayes one, and so sayes many more." This absurd notion of vicarious atonement, spun purely from Morton's imagination, appealed to Samuel Butler as worthy of further elaboration. Morton's "New English Canaan" appeared in 1632. About thirty years later the second part of the famous English satire "Hudibras" appeared, embodying Morton's idea in altered but recognizable form, in what was the most popular English book of the day. This satire, appearing when the reaction against Puritanism was at its height, was accepted and solemnly deposited at the door of the good people of Boston and Plymouth! And thus it was that Morton's fabricated tale of the Weymouth hanging passed into genuine history along with the "blue laws" of Connecticut. One cannot help believing that the mischievous perpetrator of the fable laughed up his sleeve at its result, and one cannot resist the thought that he was probably delighted to have the scandal attached to those righteous neighbors of his who had run him out of his dear Ma-re-mount.

However, driven out he was: the Maypole about which the revelers had danced was hewed down by the stern zealots who believed in dancing about only one pole, and that the whipping-post. Merrymount was deserted.

Certainly Weymouth, the honey spot which attracted not industrious bees, but only drones, was having a hard time getting settled! It was not until the Reverend Joseph Hull received permission from the General Court to settle here with twenty-one families, from Weymouth, England, that the town was at last shepherded into the Puritan fold.

These settlers, of good English stock and with the earnest ideals of pioneers, soon brought the community into good repute, and its subsequent life was as respectable and uneventful as that of a reformed *roué*. In fact there is practically no more history for Weymouth. There are certainly no more raids upon merry-makers; no more calls from the cricket colony which had sung all summer on the banks of the river to the ant colony which had providently toiled on the shore of the bay; no more experimental governments; no more scandal. The men and women of the next five generations were a poor, hard-working race, rising early and toiling late. The men worked in the fields, tending the flocks, planting and gathering the harvest. The women worked in the houses, in the dairies and kitchens, at the spinning-wheel and washtub. The privations and loneliness, which are part of every struggling colony, were augmented here, where the houses did not cluster about the church and burial ground, but were scattered and far away. This peculiarity of settlement meant much in days where there was no newspaper, no system of public transportation, no regular post, and Europe was months removed. A few of the young men went with the fishing fleet to Cape Sable, or sailed on trading vessels to the West Indies or Spain, but it is doubtful if any Weymouth-born woman ever laid eyes on the mother country during the first hundred and fifty years.

The records of the town are painfully dull. They are taken up by small domestic matters: the regulations for cattle; running boundary lines, locating highways, improving the town common, fixing fines for roving swine or agreeing to the division of a whale found on the shore. There was more or less bickering over the salary of the town clerk, who was to receive thirty-three pounds and fourteen shillings yearly to keep "A free school and teach all children and servants sent him to read and write and cast accounts."

Added to the isolation and pettiness of town affairs, the winters seem to have been longer, the snows deeper, the frosts more severe in those days. We have records of the harbor freezing over in November, and "in March the winter's snow, though much reduced, still lay on a level with the fences, nor was it until April that the ice broke up in Fore River." They were difficult—those days ushered in by the Reverend Joseph Hull. Through long nights and cold winters and an endless round of joyless living, Weymouth expiated well for the sins of her youth. Even as late as 1767 we read of the daughter of Parson Smith, of Weymouth—now the wife of John Adams, of Quincy—scrubbing the floor of her own bed-chamber the afternoon before her son—destined to become President of the United States, as his father was before him—was born.

But the English stock brought in by the Reverend Hull was good stock. We may not envy the ladies scrubbing their own floors or the men walking to Boston, but many of the best families of this country are proud to trace their origin back to Weymouth. Maine, New Hampshire, and Vermont; then New York, Rhode Island, and Connecticut attracted men from Weymouth. Later the Middle West and the Far West called them. In fact for over a century the town hardly raised its number of population, so energetic was the youth it produced.

As happens with lamentable frequency, when Weymouth ceased to be naughty she also ceased to be interesting. After poring over the dull pages of the town history, one is sometimes tempted to wonder if, perhaps, the irreverent Morton did not, for all his sins, divine a deeper meaning in this spot than the respectable ones who came after him. One cannot read the "New English Canaan" without regretting a little that this happy-natured fellow was so unceremoniously bustled out of the country. Whatever Morton's discrepancies may have been, his response to beauty was lively and true: whatever his morals, his prose is delightful. All the town records and memorial addresses of all the good folk subsequent contain no such tribute to Weymouth, and paint no picture so true of that which is still best in her, as these loving words of the erstwhile master of Merrymount.

"And when I had more seriously considered the bewty of the place, with all her fair endowments, I did not think that in all the knowne world it could be paralel'd. For so many goodly groves of trees: dainty fine round rising hillocks: delicate faire large plaines: sweete crystal fountains, and clear running streams, that twine in fine meanders through the meads, making so sweet a murmuring noise to heare, as would even lull the senses with delight asleep, so pleasantly doe they glide upon the pebble stones, jetting most jocundly where they doe meet; and hand in hand run down to Neptune's court, to pay the yearly tribute which they owe to him as soveraigne Lord of all the Springs."

CHAPTER V

ECCLESIASTICAL HINGHAM

Should you walk along the highway from Quincy to Hingham on a Sunday morning you would be passed by many automobiles, for the Old Coast Road is now one of the great pleasure highways of New England. Many of the cars are moderately priced affairs, the tonneau well filled with children of miscellaneous ages, and enlivened by a family dog or two—for this is the way that the average American household spends its modern Sabbath holiday. Now and then a limousine, exquisite in workmanship within and without, driven by a chauffeur in livery and tenanted by a single languid occupant, rolls noiselessly past. A strange procession, indeed, for a road originally marked by the moccasined feet of Indians, and widened gradually by the toilsome journeyings of rough Colonial carts and coaches.

It is difficult to say which feature of the steadily moving travel would most forcibly strike the original Puritan settlers of the town: the fact that even the common man—the poor man—could own such a vehicle of speed and ease, or the fact that America—such a short time ago a wilderness—could produce, not as the finest flower on its tree of evolution, but certainly as its most exotic, the plutocrat who lives in a palace with fifty servants to do his bidding, and the fine lady whose sole exercise of her mental and physical functions consists in allowing her maid to dress her. Yes, New England has changed amazingly in the revolutions of three centuries, and here, under the shadow of this square plain building—Hingham's Old Ship Church—while we pause to watch the Sunday pageant of 1920, we can most easily call back the Sabbath rites, and the ideals which created those rites, three centuries ago.

It is the year of 1681. This wooden meeting-house, with the truncated pyramidal roof and belfry (to serve as a lookout station), has just been built. A stage ahead, architecturally, of the log meeting-house with clay-filled chinks, thatched roof, oiled-paper windows, earthen floor, and a stage behind the charming steeple style made popular by Sir Christopher Wren, and now multiplied in countless graceful examples all over New England, the Old Ship is entirely unconscious of the distinction which is awaiting it—the distinction of being the oldest house for public worship in the United States which still stands on its original site, and which is still used for its original purpose. In the year 1681 it is merely the new meeting-house of the little hamlet of Hingham. The people are very proud of their new building. The timbers have been hewn with the broad-axe out of solid white pine (the marks are still visible, particularly in those rafters of the roof open to the attic). The belfry is precisely in the center of the four-sided pitched roof. To be sure this necessitates ringing the bell from one of the pews, but a little later the bellringer will stand above, and through a pane of glass let into the ceiling he will be able to see when the minister enters the pulpit. The original backless benches were replaced by box pews with narrow seats like shelves, hung on hinges around three sides, but part of the original pulpit remains and a few of the box pews. In 1681 the interior, like the exterior, is sternly bare. No paint, no decorations, no colored windows, no organ, or anything which could even remotely suggest the color, the beauty, the formalism of the churches of England. The unceiled roof shows the rafters whose arched timbers remind one that ships' carpenters have built this house of God.

This, then, is the meeting-house of 1681. What of the services conducted there?

In the first place, they are well attended. And why not, since in 1635 the General Court decreed that no dwelling should be placed more than half a mile away from the meeting-house of any new "plantation"—thus eliminating the excuse of too great distance? Every one is expected, nay, commanded, to come to church. In fact, after the tolling of the last bell, the houses may all be searched—each ten families is under an inspector—if there is any question of delinquents hiding in them. And so in twos and threes, often the man trudging ahead with his gun and the woman carrying her baby while the smaller children cling to her skirts, sometimes man and woman and a child or two on horseback, no matter how wild the storm, how swollen the streams, how deep the whirling snow—they all come to church: old folk and infants as well as adults and children. The congregation either waits for the minister and his wife outside the door, or stands until he has entered the pulpit. Once inside they are seated with the most meticulous exactness, according to rank, age, sex, and wealth. The small boys are separated from their families and kept in order by tithing-men who allow no wandering eyes or whispered words. The deacons are in the "fore" seats; the elderly people are sometimes given chairs at the end of the "pues"; and the slaves and Indians are in the rear. To seat one's self in the wrong "pue" is an offense punishable by a fine.

"Here is the church, and here are the people," as the old rhyme has it. What then of the services? That they are interminable we know. The tithing-man or clerk may turn the brass-bound hourglass by the side of the pulpit two and three times during the sermon, and once or twice during the prayer. Interminable, and, also, to the modern Sunday observer, unendurable. How many of us of this softer age can contemplate without a shiver the vision of people sitting hour after hour in an absolutely unheated building? (The Old Ship was not heated until 1822.) The only relief from the chill and stiffness comes during the prayer when the congregation stands: kneeling, of course, would savor too strongly of idolatry and the Church of Rome. They stand, too, while the psalms and hymns are lined out, and as they sing them, very uncertainly and very incorrectly. This performance alone sometimes takes an hour, as there is no organ, nor notes, and only a few copies of the Bay Psalm Book, of which, by the way, a copy now would be worth many times its weight in gold.

After the morning service there is a noon intermission, in which the half-frozen congregation stirs around, eats cold luncheons brought in baskets, and then returns to the next session. One must not for an instant, however, consider these noon hours as recreational. There is no idle talk or play. The sermon is discussed and the children forbidden to romp or laugh. One sometimes wonders how the little things had any impulse to laugh in such an abysmal atmosphere, but apparently the Puritan boys and girls were entirely normal and even wholesomely mischievous—as proved by the constantly required services of the tithing-man.

These external trappings of the service sound depressing enough, but if the message received within these chilly walls is cheering, maybe we can forget or ignore the physical discomforts. But is the message cheering? Hell, damnation, eternal tortures, painful theological hair-splittings, harrowing self-examinations, and humiliating public confessions—this is what they gather on the narrow wooden benches to listen to hour after hour, searching their souls for sin with an almost frenzied eagerness. And yet, forlorn and tedious as the bleak service appears to us, there is no doubt that these stern-faced men and women wrenched an almost mystical inspiration from it; that a weird fascination emanated from this morbid dwelling on sin and punishment, appealing to the emotions quite as vividly—although through a different channel—as the most elaborate ceremonial. When the soul is wrought to a certain pitch each hardship is merely an added opportunity to prove its faith. It was this high pitch, attained and sustained by our Puritan fathers, which produced a dramatic and sometimes terrible blend of personality.

It has become the modern fashion somewhat to belittle Puritanism. It is easy to emphasize its absurdities, to ridicule the almost fanatical fervor which goaded men to harshness and inconsistency. The fact remains that a tremendous selective force was needed to tear the Puritans away from the mother church and the mother country and fortify them in their struggle in a new land. It was religious zeal which furnished this motive power. Different implements and differently directed force are needed to extract the diamond from the earth, from the implements and force needed to polish and cut the same diamond. So different phases of religious development are called forth by progressive phases of development. It has been said about the New England conscience: "It fostered a condition of life and type of character doubtless never again possible in the world's history. Having done its work, having founded soundly and peopled strongly an exceptional region, the New England conscience had no further necessity for being. Those whom it now tortures with its hot pincers of doubt and self-reproach are sacrificed to a cause long since won."

The Puritans themselves grew away from many of their excessive severities. But as they gained bodily strength from their conflict with the elements, so they gained a certain moral stamina by their self-imposed religious observance. And this moral stamina has marked New England ever since, and marked her to her glory.

One cannot speak of Hingham churches—indeed, one cannot speak of Hingham—without admiring mention of the New North Church. This building, of exquisite proportions and finish, within and without, built by Bulfinch in 1806, is one of the most flawless examples of its type on the South Shore. You will appreciate the cream-colored paint, the buff walls, the quaint box pews of oiled wood, with handrails gleaming from the touch of many generations, with wooden buttons and protruding hinges proclaiming an ancient fashion; but the unique feature of the New North Church is its slave galleries. These two small galleries, between the roof and the choir loft, held for thirty years, in diminishing numbers, negroes and Indians. The last occupant was a black Lucretia, who, after being freed, was invited to sit downstairs with her master and mistress, which she did, and which she continued to do until her death, not so very long ago.

Hingham, its Main Street—alas for the original name of "Bachelors Rowe"—arched by a double row of superb elms on either side, is incalculably rich in old houses, old traditions, old families. Even motoring through, too quickly as motorists must, one cannot help being struck by the substantial dignity of the place, by the well-kept prosperity of the houses, large and small, which fringe the fine old highway. Ever since the days when the three Misses Barker kept loyal to George IV, claiming the King as their liege lord fifty years after the Declaration of Independence, the town has preserved a Cranford-like charm. And why not, when the very house is still handsomely preserved, where the nameless nobleman, Francis Le Baron, was concealed between the floors, and, as we are told in Mrs. Austen's novel, very properly capped the climax by marrying his brave little protector, Molly Wilder? Why not, when the Lincoln family, ancestors of Abraham, has been identified with the town since its settlement? The house of Major-General Benjamin Lincoln, who received the sword of Cornwallis at Yorktown, is still occupied by his descendants, its neat fence, many windows, two chimneys, and its two stories and a half proclaiming it a dwelling of repute. Near by, descendants of Samuel Lincoln, the ancestor of Abraham, occupy part of another roomy ancient homestead. The Wampatuck Club, named after the Indian chief who granted the original deeds of the town, has found quarters in an extremely interesting house dating from 1680. In the spacious living-room are seventeen panels, on the walls and in the doors, painted with charming old-fashioned skill by John Hazlitt, the brother of the English essayist. The Reverend Daniel Shute house, built in 1746, is practically intact with its paneled rooms and wallpaper a hundred years old. Hingham's famous elms shade the house where Parson Ebenezer Gay lived out his long pastorate of sixty-nine years and nine months, and the Garrison house, built before 1640, sheltered, in its prime, nine generations of the same family. The Rainbow Roof house, so called from the delicious curve in its roof, is one of Hingham's prettiest two-hundred-year-old cottages, and Miss Susan B. Willard's cottage is one of the oldest in the United States. Derby Academy, founded almost two centuries and a half ago by Madam Derby, still maintains its social and scholarly prestige through all the educational turmoil of the twentieth century. One likes to associate Hingham with Massachusetts's stanch and sturdy "war governor," for it was here that John Albion Andrew, who proved himself so truly one of our great men during the Civil War, courted Eliza Jones Hersey, and here that the happy years of their early married life were spent. Later, another governor,

John D. Long, was for many years a mighty figure in the town.

With its ancient churches and institutions, its pensive graveyards and lovely elms, its ancestral houses and hidden gardens, Hingham typifies what is quaintest and best in New England towns. Possibly the dappling of the elms, possibly the shadow of the Old Ship Church, is a bit deeper here than in the other South Shore towns. However it may seem to its inhabitants, to the stranger everything in Hingham is tinctured by the remembrance of the stern old ecclesiasticism. Even the number of historic forts seems a proper part of those righteous days, for when did religion and warfare not go hand in hand? During the trouble with King Philip the town had three forts, one at Fort Hill, one at the Cemetery, and one "on the plain about a mile from the harbor"; and the sites may still be identified.

Not that Hingham history is exclusively religious or martial. Her little harbor once held seventy sail of fishing vessels, and between 1815 and 1826, 165,000 barrels of mackerel were landed on their salty decks. For fifty years (between 1811 and 1860) the Rapid sailed as a packet between this town and Boston, making the trip on one memorable occasion in sixty-seven minutes. We read that in the War of 1812 she was carried up the Weymouth River and covered, masts and hull, with green bushes so that the marauding British cruisers might not find her, and as we read we find ourselves remembering that *camouflage* is new only in name.

How entirely fitting it seems that a town of such venerable houses and venerable legends should be presided over by a church which is the oldest of its kind in the country!

Hingham changes. There is a Roman Catholic Church in the very heart of that one-time Puritan stronghold: the New North is Unitarian, and Episcopalians, Baptists, and Second Adventists have settled down comfortably where once they would have been run out of town. Poor old Puritans, how grieved and scandalized they would be to stand, as we are standing now, and watch the procession of passing automobilists! Would it seem all lost to them, we wonder, the religious ideal for which they struggled, or would they realize that their sowing had brought forth richer fruit than they could guess? It has all changed, since Puritan days, and yet, perhaps, in no other place in New England does the hand of the past lie so visibly upon the community. You cannot lift your eyes but they rest upon some building raised two centuries and more ago; the shade which ripples under your feet is cast by elms planted by that very hand of the past. Even your voice repeats the words which those old patriarchs, well versed in Biblical lore, chose for their neighborhood names. Accord Pond and Glad Tidings Plain might have been lifted from some Pilgrim's Progress, while the near-by Sea of Galilee and Jerusalem Road are from the Good Book itself.

"Which way to Egypt?" Is this an echo from that time when the Bible was the corner-stone of Church and State, of home and school?

"What's the best road to Jericho Beach?" Surely it is some grave-faced shade who calls: or is it a peal from the chimes in the Memorial Bell Tower—chimes reminiscent of old Hingham, in England? No, it is only the shouted question of the motorist, gay and prosperous, flying on his Sunday holiday through ancient Hingham town.

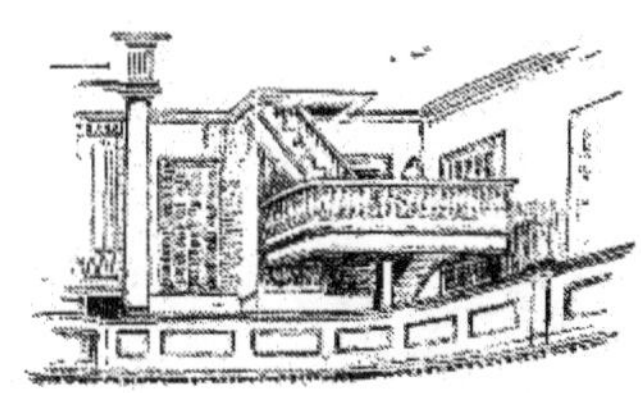

CHAPTER VI

COHASSET LEDGES AND MARSHES[1]

A sickle-shaped shore—wild, superb! Tawny ledges tumbling out to sea, rearing massive heads to search, across three thousand miles of water, for another shore. For it is Spain and Portugal which lie directly yonder, and the same tumultuous sea that crashes and swirls against Cohasset's crags laps also on those sunnier, warmer sands.

Back inland, from the bold brown coast which gives Cohasset her Riviera-like fame, lie marshes, liquefying into mirrors at high tide, melting into lush green at low tide.

Between the ledges and the marshes winds Jerusalem Road, bearing a continual stream of sight-seers and fringed with estates hidden from the sight-seers; estates with terraces dashed by spindrift, with curving stairways hewn in sheer rock down to the water, with wind-twisted savins, and flowers whose bright bloom is heightened by the tang of salt. For too many a passing traveler Cohasset is known only as the most fashionable resort on the South Shore. But Cohasset's story is a longer one than that, and far more profound.

Cohasset is founded upon a rock, and the making of that rock is so honestly and minutely recorded by nature that even those who take alarm at the word "geology" may read this record with ease. These rocky ledges that stare so proudly across the sea underlie, also, every inch of soil, and are of the same kind everywhere—granite. Granite is a rock which is formed under immense pressure and in the presence of confined moisture, needing a weight of fifteen thousand pounds upon every inch. Therefore, wherever granite is found we know that it has not been formed by deposit, like limestone and sandstone and slate and other sedimentary rocks, but at a prodigious depth under the solid ground, and by slow crystallizing of molten substances. There must have been from two to five miles of other rock lying upon the stuff that crystallized into granite. A wrinkling in the skin of the earth exposed the granite, a wrinkling so gradual that doubtless if generations of men had lived on top of the wrinkle they would have sworn it did not move. But move it did, and the superimposed rock must have been worn off at a rate of less than a hundredth part of an inch every year in order to lose two or three miles of it in twenty-five million years. As the granite was wrinkled up by the movement of the earth's crust, certain cracks opened and filled with lava, forming dikes. The geologist to-day can glance at these dikes and tell the period of their formation as casually as a jockey looking at a horse's mouth can tell his age. He could also tell of the "faulting," or slipping down, of adjacent masses of solid rock, which has occurred often enough to carve the characteristic Cohasset coast.

The making of the rock bottom is a story which extends over millions of years: the making of the soil extends over thousands. The gigantic glacier which once formed all over the northern part of North America, and which remained upon it most of the time until about seven thousand years ago, ground up the rock like a huge mill and heaped its grist into hills and plains and meadows. The marks of it are as easy to see as finger prints in putty. There are scratches on the underlying rock in every part of the town, pointing in the southerly direction in which the glacier moved. The gravel and clay belts of the town have all been stretched out in the same direction as the scratches, and many are the boulders which were combed out of the moving glacier by the peaks of the ledges, and are now poised, like the famous Tipping Rock, just where the glacier left them when it melted. Few towns in America possess greater geological interest or a wider variety of glacial phenomena than Cohasset—all of which may be studied more fully with the aid of E. Victor Bigelow's "Narrative History of the Town of Cohasset, Massachusetts," and William O. Crosby's "Geology of the Boston Basin."

This, then, is briefly the first part of Cohasset's ledges. The second part deals with human events, including many shipwrecks and disasters, and more than one romantic episode. Perhaps this human section is best begun with Captain John Smith.

Captain John Smith was born too early. If ever a hero was brought into the world to adorn the moving-picture screen, that hero of the "iron collar," of piratical capture, of wedlock with an Indian princess, was the man. Failing of this high calling he did some serviceable work in discovering and describing many of the inlets on the coast of New England. Among these inlets Cohasset acted her part as hostess to the famous navigator and staged a small and vivid encounter with the aborigines. The date of this presentation was in 1614; the scenario may be found in Smith's own diary. Smith and a party of eight or more sailors made the trip between the ledges in a small rowboat. It is believed that they landed somewhere near Hominy Point. Their landing was not carried out without some misadventure, however, for in some way this party of explorers angered the Indians with whom they came in contact, and the result was an attack from bow and arrow. The town of Cohasset, in commemorating this encounter by a tablet, has inscribed upon the tablet Smith's own words:

"We found the people on those parts very kind, but in their fury no less valiant: and at Quonhaset falling out there with but one of them, he with three others crossed the harbour in a cannow to certain rocks whereby we must pass, and there let flie their arrowes for our shot, till we were out of danger, yet one of them was slaine, and the other shot through the thigh."

History follows fast along the ledges: history of gallant deeds and gallant defense during the days of the Revolution and the War of 1812; deeds of disaster along the coast and one especial deed of great engineering skill.

The beauty and the tragedy of Cohasset are caught in large measure upon these jagged rocks. The splinters and wrecks of two and a half centuries have strewn the beaches, and many a corpse, far from its native land, has been found, wrapped in a shroud of seaweed upon the sand, and has been lowered by alien hands into a forever unmarked grave. Quite naturally the business of "wrecking"—that is, saving the pieces—came to be the trade of a number of Cohasset citizens, and so expert did Cohasset divers and seamen become that they were in demand all over the world. One of the most interesting salvage enterprises concerned a Spanish frigate, sunk off the coast of Venezuela. Many thousand dollars in silver coin were covered by fifty feet of water, and it was Captain Tower, of Cohasset, with a crew of Cohasset divers and seamen, who set sail for the spot in a schooner bearing the substantial name of Eliza Ann. The Spanish Government, having no faith in the enterprise, agreed to claim only two and one half per cent of what was removed. The first year the wreckers got fourteen thousand dollars, and the second they had reached seven thousand, when the Spaniards became so jealous of their skill that they had to flee for their lives (taking the seven thousand, however). The clumsy diving-bell method was the only one known at that time, but when, twenty years later, the Spaniards had to swallow their chagrin and send again for the same wrecking party to assist them on the same task, modern diving suits were in use and more money was recovered—no mean triumph for the crew of the Eliza Ann!

As the wrecks along the Cohasset coast were principally caused by the dangerous reefs spreading in either direction from what is known as Minot's Ledge, the necessity of a lighthouse on that spot was early evident, and the erecting of the present Minot's Light is one of the most romantic engineering enterprises of our coast history. The original structure was snapped off like a pikestaff in the great storm of 1851, and the present one of Quincy granite is the first of its kind in America to be built on a ledge awash at high tide and with no adjacent dry land. The tremendous difficulties were finally overcome, although in the year 1855 the work could be pursued for only a hundred and thirty hours, and the following year for only a hundred and fifty-seven. To read of the erection of this remarkable lighthouse reminds one of the building of Solomon's temple. The stone was selected with the utmost care, and the Quincy cutters declared that such chiseling had never before left the hand of man. Then every single block for the lower portion was meticulously cut, dovetailed, and set in position on Government Island in Cohasset Harbor. The old base, exquisitely laid, where they were thus set up is still visible, as smooth as a billiard table, although grass-covered. In addition to the flawless cutting and joining of the blocks, the ledge itself was cut into a succession of levels suitable to bear a stone foundation—work which was possible only at certain times of the tide and seasons of the year. The cutting of each stone so that it exactly fitted its neighbor, above, below, and at either side, and precisely conformed to the next inner row upon the same level, was nothing short of a marvel. A miniature of the light—the building of which took two winters, and which was on the scale of an inch to a foot—was in the United States Government Building at the Chicago Exposition, and is stone for stone a counterpart of the granite tower in the Atlantic. Although this is an achievement which belongs in a sense to the whole United States, yet it must always seem, to those who followed it most closely, as belonging peculiarly to Cohasset. A famous Cohasset rigger made the model for the derrick which was used to raise the stones; the massive granite blocks were teamed by one whose proud boast it was that he had never had occasion to shift a stone twice; a Cohasset man captained the first vessel to carry the stone to the ledge, and another assisted in the selection of the stone.

It is difficult to turn one's eyes away from the spectacular beauty of the Cohasset shore, but magnificent as these ledges are, and glittering with infinite romance, yet, rather curiously, it is on the limpid surface of the marshes that we read the most significant episodes of Colonial and pioneer life.

One of the needs which the early settlers were quick to feel was open land which would serve as pasturage for their cattle. With forests pressing down upon them from the rear, and a barrier of granite in front of them, the problem of grazing-lands was important. The Hingham settlement at Bare Cove (Cohasset was part of Hingham originally) found the solution in the acres of open marshland which stretched to the east. Cohasset to-day may ask where so much grazing-land lay within her borders. By comparison with the old maps and surveying figures, we find that many acres, now covered with the water of Little Harbor and lying within the sandbar at Pleasant Beach, are counted as old grazing-lands. These, with the sweep of what is now the "Glades," furnished abundant pasturage for neighboring cattle and brought the Hingham settlers quickly to Cohasset meadows. Thus it happens that the first history of Cohasset is the history of this common pasturage—"Commons," as it was known in the old histories. Although Hingham was early divided up among the pioneers, the marshes were kept undivided for the use of the whole settlement. As a record of 1650 puts it: "It was ordered that any townsman shall have the liberty to put swine to Conohasset without yokes or rings, upon the town's common land."

But the Massachusetts Bay Colony was hard-headed as well as pious, and several naïve hints creep into the early records of sharers of the Commons who were shrewdly eyeing the salt land of Cohasset. A real estate transfer of 1640 has this potential flavor: "Half the lot at Conehasset, if any fall by lot, and half the commons which belong to said lot." And again, four years later, Henry Tuttle sold to John Fearing "what right he had to the Division of Conihassett Meadows." The first land to come under the measuring chain and wooden stake of surveyors was about the margin of Little Harbor about the middle of the seventeenth century. After that the rest of the township was not long in being parceled out. One of the curious methods of land division was in the Beechwood district. The apportionment seems to have had the characteristics of ribbon cake. Sections of differing desirability—to meet the demands of justice and natural conditions—were measured out in long strips, a mile long and twenty-five feet wide. Many an old stone wall marking this early grant is still to be seen in the woods. Could anything but the indomitable spirit of those English settlers and the strong feeling for land ownership have built walls of carted stone about enclosures a mile long and twenty-five feet wide?

Having effected a division of land in Cohasset, families soon began to settle away from the mother town of Hingham, and after a prolonged period of government at arm's length, with all its attendant discomforts, the long, bitter struggle resolved itself into Cohasset's final separation from Hingham, and its development from a precinct into an independent township.

While the marshes to the north were the cause of Cohasset being first visited, settled, and made into a township, yet the marshes to the south hold an even more vital historical interest. These southern marshes, bordering Bound Brook and stretching away to Bassing Beach, were visited by haymakers as were those to the north. But these haymakers did not come from the same township, nor were they under the same local government. The obscure little stream which to-day lies between Scituate Harbor and Cohasset marks the line of two conflicting grants—the Plymouth Colony and the Massachusetts Bay Colony.

In the early days of New England royal grants from the throne or patents from colonial councils in London were deemed necessary before settling in the wilderness. The strong, inherited respect for landed estates must have given such charters their value, as it is hard for us to see now how any one in England could have prevented the pioneers from settling where they pleased. The various patents and grants of the two colonies (indefinite as they seem to us now, as some granted "up to" a hundred acres to each emigrant without defining any boundaries) brought the two colonies face to face at Bound Brook. The result was a dispute over the harvesting of salt hay.

All boundary streams attract to themselves a certain amount of fame—the Rio Grande, the Saint Lawrence, and the Rhine. But surely the little stream of Bound Brook, which was finally taken as the line of division between two colonies of such historical importance as the Plymouth and the Massachusetts Bay, is worth more than a superficial attention. The dispute lasted many years and occasioned the appointing of numerous commissioners from both sides. That the salt grass of Bassing Beach should have assumed such importance reveals again the sensitiveness to land values of men who had so recently left

England. The settling of the dispute was not referred back to England, but was settled by the colonists themselves.

The author of the "Narrative History of Cohasset" calls this an event of only less historical importance than that of the pact drawn up in the cabin of the Mayflower. He declares that the confederation of states had its inception there, and adds: "The appointment for this joint commission for the settlement of this intercolonial difficulty was the first step of federation that culminated in the Colonial Congress and then blossomed into the United States." We to-day, to whom the salt grass of Cohasset is little more than a fringe about the two harbors, may find it difficult to agree fully with such a sweeping statement, but certainly this spot and boundary line should always be associated with the respect for property which has ennobled the Anglo-Saxon race.

Between the marshes, which were of such high importance in those early days, and the ledges which have been the cause and the scene of so many Cohasset adventures, twists Jerusalem Road, the brilliant beauty of which has been so often—but never too often—remarked. This was the main road from Hingham for many years, and it took full three hours of barbarous jolting in two-wheeled, springless ox carts to make the trip. Even if a man had a horse the journey was cruelly tedious, for there were only a few stretches where the horse could go faster than a walk—and the way was pock-marked with boulders and mudholes. With no stage-coach before 1815, and being off the highway between Plymouth and Boston, it is small wonder that the early Cohasset folk either walked or went by sea to Hingham and thence to Boston.

It has been suggested that the "keeper of young cattle at Coneyhassett," who drove his herd over from Hingham, was moved either by piety or sarcasm to give the trail its present arresting name. However, as the herdsman did not take this route, but the back road through Turkey Meadows, it is more probable that some visitors, who detected a resemblance between this section of the country and the Holy Land, were responsible for the christening of this road and also of the Sea of Galilee—which last has almost dropped into disuse. There does not seem to be any particular suggestion of the land of the Pharaohs and present-day Egypt, but tradition explains that as follows: Old Squire Perce had accumulated a store of grain in case of drought, and when the drought came and the men hurried to him to buy corn, he greeted them with "Well, boys, so you've come down to Egypt to buy corn." Another proof, if one were needed, of the Biblical familiarity of those days.

It is hard to stop writing about Cohasset. There are so many bits of history tucked into every ledge and cranny of her shore. The green in front of the old white meeting-house—one of the prettiest and most perfect meeting-houses on the South Shore—has been pressed by the feet of men assembling for six wars. It makes Cohasset seem venerable, indeed, when one thinks of the march of American history. But to the tawny ledges, tumbling out to sea, these three hundred years are as but a day; for the story of the stones, like the story of the stars, is measured in terms of milliards. To such immemorial keepers of the coast the life of man is a brief tale that is soon told, and fades as swiftly as the fading leaf.

FOOTNOTES:

[1] For much of this chapter I am indebted to my friend Alice C. Hyde.

CHAPTER VII

THE SCITUATE SHORE

Scituate is different: different from Cohasset, with its superbly bold coast and its fashionable folk; different from Hingham, with its air of settled inland dignity. Scituate has a quaintness, a casualness, the indescribable air of a land's-end spot. The fine houses in Scituate are refreshingly free from pretension; the winds that have twisted the trees into Rackham-like grotesques have blown away falsity and formality.

Scituate life has always been along the shore. It is from the shore that coot-shooting used to furnish a livelihood to many a Scituate man, and still lures the huntsmen in the fine fall weather. It is the peculiar formation of the shore which has developed a small, clinker-built boat, and made the town famous for day fishing. It is along the shore that the unique and picturesque mossing industry is still carried on, and along the shore that the well-known colony of literary folk have settled.

Scituate's history is really a fishing history, for as early as 1633 a fishing station was established here, and in course of time the North River, winding twenty miles through green meadows to the sea, was once the scene of more shipbuilding than any other river in New England.

There is nothing more indicative of the Yankees' shrewd practicality than the early settlers' instant appreciation of the financial and economic potentialities of the fishing-trade. The Spaniard sought for gold in the new country, or contented himself with the fluctuating fur trade with its demoralizing slack seasons. But the New Englander promptly applied himself to the mundane pursuit of cod and mackerel. Everybody fished. As John Smith, in his "Description of New England," says: "Young boyes and girles, salvages or any other, be they never such idlers, may turne, carry, and returne fish without shame or either great pain: he is very idle that is past twelve years of age and cannot doe so much: and shee is very old that cannot spin a thread to catch them."

It began when Squanto the Indian showed the amazed colonists how he could tread the eels out of the mud with his feet and catch them with his hands. This was convenient, to be sure, but the colonists did not long content themselves with such primitive methods. They sent to England for cod hooks and lines; mackerel hooks and lines; herring nets and seines; shark hooks, bass nets, squid lines, and eel pots; and in a short time they had established a trade which meant more money than the gold mines of Guiana or Potosi. The modern financier who makes a fortune from the invention of a collar button or the sale of countless penny packages of gum is the lineal descendant of that first thrifty New Englander who did not scorn the humble cod because it was cheap and plentiful (you remember how these same cod "pestered" the ships of Gosnold in 1602), but set to work with the quiet initiative which has distinguished New Englanders ever since, first to catch, then to barter, and finally to sell his wares to all the world. For cheap as all fish was—twopence for a twelve-pound cod, salmon less than a penny a pound, and shad, when it was finally considered fit to eat at all, at two fish for a penny—yet, when all the world is ready to buy and the supply is inexhaustible, tremendous profits are possible. The many fast days of the Roman Catholic Church abroad opened an immense demand, and in a short time quantities of various kinds of fish (Josselyn in 1672 enumerates over two hundred caught in New England waters) were dried and salted and sent to England.

This constant and steadily increasing trade radically affected the whole economic structure and history of New England for two centuries. Ships and all the shipyard industries; the farm, on which fish was used not only as a medium of exchange, but also as a valuable fertilizer; the home, where the many operations of curing and salting were carried on—all of those were developed directly by the growth of this particular trade. Laws were made and continually revised regarding the fisheries and safeguarding their rights in every conceivable fashion; ship carpenters were exempt from military service, and many special exemptions were extended to fishermen under the general statutes.

The oyster is now a dish for the epicure and the lobster for the millionaire. But in the old days when oysters a foot long were not uncommon, and lobsters sometimes grew to six feet, every one had all he wanted, and sometimes more than he wanted, of these delicacies. The stranger in New England may notice how certain customs still prevail, such as the Friday night fish dinner and the Sunday morning fish-cakes; and also that New Englanders as a whole have a rather fastidious taste in regard to the preparation of both salt- and fresh-water products. The food of any region is characteristic of that region, and to travel along the Old Coast Road and not partake of one of the delicious fish dinners, is as absurd as it would be to omit rice from a menu in China or roast beef from an English dinner.

While the fishing trade was highly important in all the South Shore towns, yet it was especially so in Scituate. In 1770 more than thirty vessels, principally for mackerel, were fitted out in this one village, and these vessels not infrequently took a thousand barrels in a season. In winter they were used for Southern coasting, carrying lumber and fish and returning with grain and flour. The reason why fishing was so persistently and exclusively followed in this particular spot is not hard to seek. The sea yielded a far more profitable and ready crop than the land, and, besides, had a jealous way of nibbling away at the land wherever it could. It is estimated that it wastes away from twelve to fourteen inches of Fourth Cliff every year.

But in spite of the sea's readily accessible crop it was natural that the "men of Kent" who settled the town should demand some portion of dry land as well. These men of Kent were not mermen, able to live in and on the water indefinitely, but decidedly gallant fellows, rather more courtly than their neighbors, and more polished than the race which succeeded them. Gilson, Vassal, Hatherly, Cudworth, Tilden, Hoar, Foster, Stedman, and Hinckley had all been accustomed to the elegancies of life in England as their names testify. The first land they used was on the cliffs, for it had already been improved by Indian planting; then the salt marshes, covered with a natural crop of grass, and then the mellow intervales near the river. When the sea was forced to the regretful realization that she could not monopolize the entire attention of her fellows, she was persuaded to yield up some very excellent fertilizer in the way of seaweed. But she still nags away at the cliffs and shore, and proclaims with every flaunting wave and ripple that it is the water, not the land, which makes Scituate what it is.

And, after all, the sea is right. It is along the shore that one sees Scituate most truly. Here the characteristic industry of mossing is still carried on in primitive fashion. The mossers work from dories, gathering with long-handled rakes the seaweed from the rocks and ledges along the shore. They bring it in, a heavy, dark, inert mass, all sleek and dripping, and spread it out to dry in the sun. As it lies there, neatly arranged on beds of smoothest pebbles, the sun bleaches it. One can easily differentiate the different days' haul, for the moss which is just spread out is almost black and that of yesterday is a dark purple. It shimmers from purple into lavender; the lavender into something like rose; and by the time of the final washing and bleaching it lies in fine light white crinkles, almost like wool. It is a pretty sight, and the neatness and dispatch of the mossers make the odd sea-flower gardens attractive patches on the beach. Sometimes a family working together will make as much as a thousand dollars in a season gathering and preparing the moss. One wonders if all the people in the world could eat enough blancmange to consume this salty product, and is relieved to be reminded that the moss is also used for brewing and dyeing.

It is really a pity to see Scituate only from a motor. There is real atmosphere to the place, which is worth breathing, but it takes more time to breathe in an atmosphere than merely to "take the air." Should you decide to ramble about the ancient town you will surely find your way to Scituate Point. The old stone lighthouse, over a century old, is no longer used, and the oil lantern, hung nightly out at the end of the romantic promontory, seems a return to days of long ago. You will also see the place where, in the stirring Revolutionary days, little Abigail and Rebecca Bates, with fife and drum marched up and down, close to the shore and yet hidden from sight, playing so furiously that their "martial music and other noises" scared away the enemy and saved the town from invasion. You will go to Second Cliff where are the summer homes of many literary people, and you will pass through Egypt, catching what glimpse you can of the stables and offices, paddocks and cottages of the immense estate of Dreamwold. And of course you will have pointed out to you the birthplace of Samuel Woodworth, whose sole claim to remembrance is his poem of the "Old Oaken Bucket." The well-sweep is still where he saw it, when, as editor of the *New York Mirror*, it suddenly flashed before his reminiscent vision, but the old oaken bucket itself has been removed to a museum.

After you have done all these things, you will, if you are wise, forsake Scituate Harbor, which is the old section, and Scituate Beach, which is the newer, summer section, and find the way to the burial ground, which, after the one in Plymouth, is the oldest in the State. Possibly there will be others at the burial ground, for ancestor worshipers are not confined to China, and every year there springs up a new crop of genealogists to kneel before the moss-grown headstones and, with truly admirable patience, decipher names and dates, half obliterated by the finger of time. One does not wonder that their descendants are so eager to trace their connection back to those men of Kent, whose sturdy title rings so bravely down the centuries. To be sure, what is left to trace is very slight in most cases, and quite without any savor of personality. Too often it is merely brief and dry recital of dates and number of progeny, and names of the same. Few have left anything so quaint as the words of Walter Briggs, who settled there in 1651 and from whom Briggs Harbor was named. His will contains this thoughtful provision: "For my wife Francis, one third of my estate during her life, also a gentle horse or mare, and Jemmy the negur shall catch it for her."

The good people who came later (1634) from Plymouth and Boston and took up their difficult colonial life under the pastorate of Mr. Lathrop, seem to have done their best to make "Satuit" (as it was first called, from the Indians, meaning "cold brook") conform as nearly as possible to the other pioneer settlements, even to the point of discovering witches here. But religion and fasting were not able to accomplish what the ubiquitous summer influx has, happily, also failed to effect. Scituate remains different.

Perhaps it was those men of Kent who gave it its indestructibly romantic bias; perhaps it is the jealousy of the ever-encroaching sea. The gray geese flying over the iridescent moss gleaming upon the pebbled beaches, the solitary lantern on the point are all parts of that differentness. And those who love her best are glad that it is so.

CHAPTER VIII

MARSHFIELD, THE HOME OF DANIEL WEBSTER

Ye marshes, how candid and simple and nothing-withholding and free!
Ye publish yourselves to the sky and offer yourselves to the sea!
Tolerant plains, that suffer the sea and the rains and the sun,
Ye spread and span like the catholic man who hath mightily won
God out of knowledge, and good out of infinite pain,
And sight out of blindness, and purity out of a stain.

It was these mighty marshes—this ample sweep of grass, of sea and sky—this vast earthly and heavenly spaciousness that must forever stand to all New Englanders as a background to the powerful personality who chose it as his own home. Daniel Webster, when his eyes first turned to this infinite reach of largeness, instinctively knew it as the place where his splendid senses would find satisfaction, and his splendid mind would soar into an even loftier freedom. Webster loved Marshfield with an intensity that made it peculiarly his own. Lanier, in language more intricate and tropical, exclaimed of his "dim sweet" woods: "Ye held me fast in your heart, and I held you fast in mine." Webster wielded the vital union between his nature and that of the land not only by profound sentiment, but by a vigorous physical grappling with the soil.

Is it that vivid natures unconsciously seek an environment characteristic of them? Or are they, perhaps, inevitably forced to create such an environment wherever they find themselves? Both facts seem true in this case. This wide world of marsh and sea is not only beautifully expressive of one who plunged himself into a rich communion with the earth, with her full harvests and blooded cattle, with her fruitful brooks and lakes; but it is still, after more than half a century, vibrant with the spirit of the man who dwelt there.

We of another generation—and a generation before whom so many portentous events and figures have passed—find it hard to realize the tremendous magnetism and brilliancy of a man who has been so long dead, or properly to estimate the high historical significance of such a life.

The human attribute which is the most immediately impelling in direct intercourse—personality—is the most elusive to preserve. If Webster's claim to remembrance rested solely upon that attribute, he would still be worthy of enduring fame. But his gifts flowered at a spectacular climax of national affairs and won thereby spectacular prominence. That these gifts were to lose something of their pristine repute before the end infuses, from a dramatic point of view, a contrasted and heightened luster to the period of their highest glory.

Let us, casual travelers of a later and more careless day, walk now together over the place which is the indestructible memorial of a great man, and putting aside the measuring-stick of criticism—the sign of small natures—try to live for an hour in the atmosphere which was the breath of life to one who, if he failed greatly, also succeeded greatly, and whose noble achievement it was not only to express, but to vivify a love for the Union which, in its hour of supreme trial, became its triumphant force.

Could we go back—not quite a hundred years—a little off the direct route to Plymouth, on a site overlooking the broad marshes of Green Harbor and the sea, where there now stands a boulder erected in 1914 by the Boston University Law School Association, we would find a comfortable, rambling house, distinguished among its New England neighbors by an easy and delightful hospitality—the kind of hospitality we call "Southern." There are many people in the house, on the veranda and lawns: a hostess of gentle mien and manners; children attractive in the spontaneity of those who continually and happily associate with their elders; several house guests (yonder is Audubon the great naturalist, here is an office-seeker from Boston, and that chap over there, so very much at home, can be no other than Peter Harvey, Webster's fond biographer). Callers there are, also, as is shown by the line of chaises and saddle horses waiting outside, and old Captain Thomas and his wife, from whom the place was bought, and who still retain their original quarters, move in and out like people who consider themselves part of the family. It is a heterogeneous collection, yet by no means an awkward one, and every one is chatting with every one else with great amiability. It is late afternoon: the master of the house has been away all day, and now his guests and his family are glancing in the direction from which he may be expected. For although every one is comfortable and properly entertained, yet the absence of the host creates an inexpressible emptiness; it is as if everything were quiescent—hardly breathing—merely waiting until he comes. Suddenly the atmosphere changes; it is charged with a strong vibrant quality; everything—all eyes, all interest—is instantly focused on the figure which has appeared among them. He is in fisherman's clothes—this newcomer—attired with a brave eye for the picturesque, in soft hat and flowing tie; but there are no fisherman's clothes, no, nor any other cloakings which can conceal the resilient dignity of his bearing, his impressive build, and magnificent, kingly head. Sydney Smith called Webster a cathedral; and surely there must have been something in those enormous, burning eyes, that craglike brow, that smote even the most superficial observer into an admiration which was almost awe.

Many men—perhaps even the majority—whatever their genius in the outer world, in their own houses are either relegated to—or choose—the inconspicuous rôle of mere masculine appendages. But here we have a man who is superbly the host: he knows and welcomes every guest and caller; he personally supervises the disposal of their baggage and the selection of their chambers; he himself has ordered the dinner—mutton which he has raised, fish which he has caught—and it is being cooked by Monica, the Southern slave whose freedom he purchased for her. He carves at table, priding himself on his dispatch and nicety, and keeps an eye on the needs of every one at the long board. Everything, every one in the house is irresistibly drawn about this magnetic center which dominates by its innate power of personality more than by any deliberate intention. His children worship him; his wife idolizes him; each man and woman on the place regards him with admiring affection. And in such congenial atmosphere he expands, is genial, kindly, delightful. But devoted as he is to his home, his family, and his friends, and charming as he shows himself with them, yet it is not until we see him striding over the farm which he has bought that we see the Daniel Webster who is destined to live most graphically in the memories of those who like to think of great men in those intimate moments which are most personally characteristic of them.

We must rise early in the morning if we would accompany him on his day's round. He himself is up at sunrise, for the sunrise is to him signal to new life. As he once wrote: "Among all our good people not one in a thousand sees the sun rise once a year. They know nothing of the morning. Their idea of it is that part of the day which comes along after a cup of coffee and a beefsteak or a piece of toast. With them morning is not a new issuing of light, a new bursting forth of the sun, a new waking up of all that has life from a sort of temporary death, to behold again the works of God, the heavens and the earth.... The first faint streak of light, the earliest purpling of the east which the lark springs up to greet, and the deeper and deeper coloring into orange and red, till at length the 'glorious sun is seen, regent of the day'—this they never enjoy, for they never see it."

So four o'clock finds Webster up and dressed and bound for the little study in his garden (the only building spared by the fire which destroyed the house in 1878) and beginning his correspondence. If he has no secretary he writes himself, and by time breakfast is announced twenty letters, all franked and sealed, are ready to be posted.

"Now," he says, smiling benignantly down the long breakfast table of family and friends, "my day's work is done—I have nothing to do but fish."

Although this is, indeed, his favorite sport, and there is hardly a brook or lake or pond within a radius of twenty miles which does not bear the charmed legend of having been one of his favorite fishing grounds, he does not spend his days in amusement, like the typical country gentleman. Farming to him, the son of a yeoman, is no mere possession of a fine estate, but the actual participation in ploughing, planting, and haying. His full animal spirits find relief in such labor. We cannot think of any similar example of such prodigious mental and physical energy. Macaulay was a great parliamentary orator, but he was the most conventional of city men; Burke and Chatham had no strength for such strenuousness after their professional toil. But Webster loved to know and to put his hand to every detail of farming and stock-raising. When he first came to Marshfield the soil was thin and sandy. It was he who instituted scientific farming in the region, teaching the natives how to fertilize with kelp which was easily obtainable from the sea, and also with the plentiful small herring or menhaden. He taught them the proper care of the soil, and the rotation of crops. This passionate love of the earth was an integral part of the man. As the force of his mind drew its power, not from mere rhetorical facility, but from fundamental principles, so his magnificent body, like that of the fabled Antæus, seemed to draw perennial potency from contact with the earth. To acquire land—he owned nearly eighteen hundred acres at the time of his death—and to cultivate it to the highest possible degree of productiveness was his intense delight. The farm which he purchased from Captain Thomas grew to an estate of two or three dozen buildings, outhouses, tenant houses, a dairyman's cottage, fisherman's house, agricultural offices, and several large barns. We can imagine that he shows us all of these things—explaining every detail with enthusiasm and accuracy, occasionally digressing upon the habits of birds or fish, the influence of tides and currents, the changes of sky and wind. All natural laws are fascinating to him—inspiring his imagination and uplifting his spirit—and it is these things, never politics or business, which he discusses in his hours of freedom. He himself supervises the planting and harvesting and slaughtering here and on his other farm at Franklin—the family homestead—even when obliged to be absent, or even when temporarily residing in Washington and hard pressed with the cares of his office as Secretary of State.

Those painters who include a parrot in the portrait of some fine frivolous lady do so to heighten their interpretation of character. We all betray our natures, by the creatures we instinctively gather about us. One might know that Jefferson at Monticello would select high-bred saddle horses as his companions; that Cardinal Richelieu would find no pet so soothing, so alluring, as a soft-stepping cat; that Charles I would select the long-haired spaniel. So it is entirely in the picture that of all the beasts brought under human yoke, that great oxen, slow, solemn, strong, would appeal to the man whose searching eyes were never at rest except when they swept a wide horizon; whose mind found its deepest satisfaction in noble languages, the giant monuments of literature and art, and whose soul best stretched its wings beside the limitless sea and under the limitless sky. Webster was fond of all animal life; he felt himself part of its free movement. Guinea hens, peacocks, ducks, flocks of tamed wild geese, dogs, horses—these were all part of the Marshfield place, but there was within the breast of the owner a special responsiveness to great herds of cattle, and especially fine oxen, the embodiment of massive power. So fond was he of these favorite beasts of his, that often on his arrival home he would fling his bag into the hall without even entering the house, and hasten to the barn to see that they were properly tied up for the night. As he once said to his little son, as they both stood by the stalls and he was feeding the oxen with ears of corn from an unhusked pile lying on the barn floor: "I would rather be here than in the Senate," adding, with his famous smile, "I think it is better company." So we may be sure as we walk in our retrospect about the farm with him—he never speaks of it as an "estate" but always as a farm—he will linger longest where the Devon oxen, the Alderneys, Herefordshire, and Ayrshire are grazing, and that the eyes which Carlyle likened to anthracite furnaces will glow and soften. Twenty years from now he will gaze out upon his oxen once again from the window before which he has asked to be carried, as he lies waiting for death. Weariness, disease, and disappointment have weakened the elasticity of his spirit, and as they pass—his beloved oxen, slowly, solemnly—what procession of the years passes with them! Years of full living, of generous living; of deep emotions; of glory; years of ambition; of bereavement; of grief. It is all to pass—these happy days at Marshfield; the wife he so fondly cared for; the children he so deeply cherished. Sycophants are to fill, in a measure, the place of friends, the money which now flows in so freely is to entangle and ensnare him; the lofty aspiration which now inspires him is to degenerate into a presidential ambition which will eat into his soul. But to-day let us, as long as we may, see him as he is in the height of his powers. Let us walk with him under the trees which he planted. Those large elms, gracefully silhouetted against the house, were placed there with his own hands at the birth of his son Edward and his daughter Julia, and he always refers to them gently as "brother" and "sister." To plant a tree to mark an event was one of his picturesque customs—an unconscious desire, perhaps, to project himself into the future. I am quite sure, as we accompany him, he will expatiate on the improvement in the soil which he has effected; that he will point out eagerly not only the domestic but the wild animals about the place; and that he will stand for a few moments on the high bluff overlooking the sea and the marshes and let the wind blow through his dark hair. He is carefully dressed—he always dresses to fit the occasion—and to-day, as he stands in his long boots reaching to the knee and adorned with a tassel, his bell-crowned beaver hat in his hand, and in his tight pantaloons and well-cut coat—a magnificent specimen of virile manhood—the words of Lanier, although written at a later date, and about marshes far more lush than these New England ones, beat upon our ears:

"Oh, what is abroad in the marsh and the terminal sea?
Somehow my soul seems suddenly free
From the weighing of fate and the sad discussion of sin,
By the length and the breadth and the sweep of the marshes of Glynn."

On the way back he will show us the place where three of his favorite horses are buried, for he does not sell the old horses who have done him good service, but has them buried "with the honors of war"—that is, standing upright, with their halters and shoes on. Above one of them he has placed the epitaph:

"Siste Viator!
Viator te major his sistit."

I do not know if, as we return to the house where already a fresh group of visitors has arrived, he will pause by a corner of the yard set off by an iron fence. He has chosen this spot as the place where he shall lie, and here, in time, are to repose under the wide and simple vault of sky the wife and children whose going before is to bring such desolation. It is a place supremely fitting for that ample spirit which knew for its own the nobility of large spaces, and the grandeur of repose.

The life of Daniel Webster is one of the most dramatic and touching of any of our great men. He was an orator of such solid thought and chaste eloquence that even now, without the advantage of the marvelously rich and flexible voice and the commanding presence that made each word burn like a fire, even without this incalculable personal interpretation, his speeches remain as a permanent part of our literature, and will so long as English oratory is read. He was a brilliant lawyer—the foremost of his day—and his statesmanship was of equal rank. In private life he was a peculiarly devoted and tender son, husband, father, and friend. That he should have become saddened by domestic losses and somewhat vitiated by flattery were, perhaps, inevitable. He was bitterly condemned—more bitterly by his contemporaries than by those who now study his words and work—for lowering his high standard in regard to slavery. It is impossible to refute the accusation, at the end of his life, of a carelessness approaching unscrupulousness in money matters. His personal failings, which were those of a man of exceptional vitality, have been heavily—too heavily—emphasized. He ate and drank and spent money lavishly; he had a fine library; he loved handsome plate and good service and good living. He was generous; he was kind. That he was susceptible to adulation and, after the death of his first wife, drifted into associations less admirable than those of his earlier years, are the dark threads of a woof underrunning a majestic warp. He adored his country with a fervor that savors of the heroic, and when he said, "There are no Alleghanies in my politics," he spoke the truth. The intense passion for the soil which animated him at Marshfield was only a fragment of that higher passion for his country—feeling never tainted by sectionalism or local prejudice. It was this profound love for the Union, coupled with his surpassing gift of eloquence in expressing that love and inspiring it in all who heard him, that distinguishes him for all time.

There are other memorable things about Marshfield. Governor Edward Winslow, who was sent to England to represent the Plymouth and Massachusetts Bay Colonies, and whose son Josiah was the first native Governor of the Colony, may both be called Marshfield men. Peregrine White, the first white child born in this country, lies in the Winslow Burying Ground. One of the most singular changes on our coast occurred in this vicinity when in one night the "Portland Breeze" closed up the mouth of the South River and four miles up the beach opened up the mouth of the North River, making an entrance three quarters of a mile wide between Third and Fourth Cliff.

These and many other men and events of Marshfield are properly given a place in the history of New England, but the special glory of this spot will always be that Daniel Webster chose to live, chose to die, and chose to be buried under the vast vault of her skyey spaces, within the sound of her eternal sea.

CHAPTER IX

DUXBURY HOMES

There are certain places whose happy fortune seems to be that they are always specially loved and specially sought by the children of men. From that memorable date in 1630 when a little group of the Plymouth colonists asked permission to locate across the bay at "Duxberie" until now, when the summer colony alone has far surpassed that of the original settlers, this section of the coast—with its lovely six-mile beach, its high bluffs, and its pleasant hills and pasture lands, upon which are found quite a southern flora, unique in this northern latitude—has been thoroughly frequented and enjoyed.

There is no more graphic index to the caliber of a people than the houses which they build, and the first house above all others which we must associate with this spot is the Standish cottage, built at the foot of Captain's Hill by Alexander Standish, the son of Myles, partly from materials from his father's house, which was burned down, but whose cellar is still visible. This long, low, gambrel-roofed structure, with a broad chimney showing the date of 1666, was a long way ahead of the first log cabins erected by the Pilgrims— farther than most of us realize, accustomed as we are to glass instead of oiled paper in windows; to shingles, and not thatch for roofs. It is fitting that this ancient and charming dwelling should be associated with one of the most romantic, most striking, names in the Plymouth Colony. There are few more picturesque personalities in our early history than Myles Standish. Small in stature, fiery in spirit, a terror to the Indians, and a strong arm to the Pilgrims, there is no doubt that his determination to live in Duxbury—which he named for Duxborough Hall, his ancestral home in Lancashire—went far in obtaining for it a separate incorporation and a separate church. This was the first definite offshoot from the Plymouth Colony, and was accompanied by the usual maternal fears. While he could not forbid them going to Duxbury to settle, yet, when they asked for a separate incorporation and church, Bradford granted it most unwillingly. He voiced the general sentiment when he wrote that such a separation presaged the ruin of the church "& will provoke y͡e Lord's displeasure against them."

However, such unkind predictions in no wise bothered the sturdy little group who moved over to the new location, needing room for their cattle and their gardens, and most of all a sense of freedom from the restrictions of the mother colony. The son of Elder Brewster went, and in time the Elder himself, and so did John Alden and his wife Priscilla, whose courtship has been so well told by Longfellow that it needs no further embellishing here. On the grassy knoll where John and Priscilla built their home in 1631, their grandson built the cottage which now stands—the property of the Alden Kindred Association. John Alden seems to have been an attractive young fellow—it is easy to see why Priscilla Mullins preferred him to the swart, truculent widower—but from our point of view John Alden's chief claim to fame is that he was a friend of Myles Standish.

Let us, as we pay our respects to Duxbury, pause for a moment and recall some of the courageous adventures, some of the brave traits and some of the tender ones, which make up our memory of this doughty military commander. In the first place, we must remember that he was never a member of the church of the Pilgrims: there is even a question if he were not—like the rest of his family in Lancashire—a Roman Catholic; and this immediately places him in a position of peculiar distinction. From the first his mission was not along ecclesiastical lines, but along military and civil ones. The early histories are full of his intrepid deeds: there was never an expedition too dangerous or too difficult to daunt him. He would attack with the utmost daring the hardest or the humblest task. He was absolutely loyal to the interest of the Colony, and during that first dreadful winter when he was among the very few who were not stricken with sickness, he tended the others day and night, "unceasing in his loving care." As in many audacious characters this sweeter side of his nature does not seem to have been fully appreciated by his contemporaries, and we have the letter in which Robinson, that "most learned, polished and modest spirit," writes to Bradford, and warns him to have care about Standish. He loves him right well, and is persuaded that God has given him to them in mercy and for much good, if he is used aright; but he fears that there may be wanting in him "that tenderness of the life of man (made after God's image) which is meet." This warning doubtless flattered Standish, but Robinson's later criticism of his methods at Weymouth hurt the little captain cruelly. He seems to have cherished an intense affection for the Leyden pastor, such as valorous natures often feel for meditative ones, and that Robinson died before he—Standish—could justify himself was a deep grief to the soldier to whom mere physical hardships were as nothing. We do not know a great deal about this relationship between the two men: in this as in so many cases the intimate stories of these men and women, "also their love, and their hatred, and their envy is now perished." But we do know that thirty years later when the gallant captain lay dying he wrote in his will: "I give three pounds to Mercy Robinson, whom I tenderly love for her grandfather's sake." Surely one feels the touching eloquence of this brief sentence the fitting close of a life not only heroic in action, but deeply sensitive in sentiment.

He died on his farm in Duxbury in 1656 when he was seventy-three, and the Myles Standish Monument on Captain's Hill, three hundred and ten feet above the bay, is no more conspicuous than his knightly and tender life among the people he elected to serve. His two wives, and also Priscilla and John Alden, for whom he entertained such lively love and equally lively fury, all are buried here—the Captain's last home fittingly marked by four cannon and a sturdy boulder.

Not only for Standish and Alden is Duxbury famous. The beloved William Brewster himself moved to this new settlement, and up to a few years ago the traces of the whitewood trees which gave the name of "Eagle's Nest" to his house could be distinguished. One son—Love—lived with the venerable elder, who was a widower, and his other son Jonathan owned the neighboring farm. In the sight of the Plymouth Colony—their first home in the new land—the three men often worked together, cutting trees and planting.

Others of the original Mayflower company came too, leaving traces of themselves in such names as Blackfriars Brook, Billingsgate, and Houndsditch—names which they brought from Old England.

The homes which these pioneers so laboriously and so lovingly wrought— what were they? How did they compare with the modern home and household? In Mr. Sheldon's "History of Deerfield" we find such a charming and vivid picture of home life in the early days—and one that applies with equal accuracy to Duxbury—that we cannot do better than copy it here:

"The ample kitchen was the center of the family life, social and industrial. Here around the rough table, seated on rude stools or benches, all partook of the plain and sometimes stinted fare. A glance at the family gathered here after nightfall on a winter's day may prove of interest.

"After a supper of bean porridge or hasty pudding and milk of which all partake in common from a great pewter basin, or wooden bowl, with spoons of wood, horn or pewter; after a reverent reading of the Bible, and fervent supplications to the Most High for prayer and guidance; after the watch was set on the tall mount, and the vigilant sentinel began pacing his lonely beat, the shutters were closed and barred, and with a sense of security the occupations of the long winter evening began. Here was a picture of industry enjoined alike by the law of the land and the stern necessities of the settlers. All were busy. Idleness was a crime. On the settle, or a low armchair, in the most sheltered nook, sat the revered grandam—as a term of endearment called granny—in red woolen gown, and white linen cap, her gray hair and wrinkled face reflecting the bright firelight, the long stocking growing under her busy needles, while she watched the youngling of the flock in the cradle by her side. The good wife, in linsey-woolsey short-gown and red petticoat steps lightly back and forth in calf pumps beside the great wheel, or poising gracefully on the right foot, the left hand extended with the roll or bat, while with a wheel finger in the other, she gives the wheel a few swift turns for a final twist to the long-drawn thread of wool or tow. The continuous buzz of the flax wheels, harmonizing with the spasmodic hum of the big wheel, shows that the girls are preparing a stock of linen against their wedding day. Less active and more fitful rattled the quill wheel, where the younger children are filling quills for the morrow's weaving.

"Craftsmen are still scarce, and the yeoman must depend largely on his own skill and resources. The grandsire, and the goodman, his son, in blue woolen frocks, buckskin breeches, long stockings, and clouted brogans with pewter buckles, and the older boys in shirts of brown tow, waistcoat and breeches of butternut-colored woolen homespun, surrounded by piles of white hickory shavings, are whittling out with keen Barlow jack-knives implements for home use: ox-bows and bow-pins, axe-helves, rakestales, forkstales, handles for spades and billhooks, wooden shovels, flail staff and swingle, swingling knives, or pokes and hog yokes for unruly cattle and swine. The more ingenious, perhaps, are fashioning buckets or powdering tubs, or weaving skeps, baskets or snowshoes. Some, it may be, sit astride the wooden shovel, shelling corn on its iron-shod edge, while others are pounding it into samp or hoiminy in the great wooden mortar.

"There are no lamps or candles, but the red light from the burning pine knots on the hearth glows over all, repeating, in fantastic pantomime on the brown walls and closed shutters, the varied activities around it. These are occasionally brought into higher relief by the white flashes, as the boys throw handfuls of hickory shavings onto the forestick, or punch the back log with the long iron peel, while wishing they had as 'many shillings as sparks go up the chimney.' Then, the smoke-stained joists and boards of the ceiling with the twisted rings of pumpkin strings or crimson peppers and festoons of apple, drying on poles hung beneath; the men's hats, the crook-necked squashes, the skeins of thread and yarn hanging in bunches on the wainscot; the sheen of the pewter plates and basins, standing in rows on the shelves of the dresser; the trusty firelock with powder horn, bandolier, and bullet pouch, hanging on the summertree, and the bright brass warming-pan behind the bedroom door—all stand revealed more clearly for an instant, showing the provident care for the comfort and safety of the household. Dimly seen in the corners of the room are baskets in which are packed hands of flax from the barn, where, under the flaxbrake, the swingling knives and the coarse hackle, the shives and swingling tow have been removed by the men; to-morrow the more deft manipulations of the women will prepare these bunches of fiber for the little wheel, and granny will card the tow into bats, to be spun into tow yarn on the big wheel. All quaff the sparkling cider or foaming beer from the briskly circulating pewter mug, which the last out of bed in the morning must replenish from the barrel in the cellar."

One notices the frequent reference to beer in these old chronicles. The tea, over which the colonists were to take such a dramatic stand in a hundred years, had not yet been introduced into England, and neither had coffee.

Forks had not yet made their appearance. In this admirable picture Mr. Sheldon does not mention one of the evening industries which was peculiarly characteristic of the Plymouth Colony. This was the making of clapboards, which with sassafras and beaver skins, constituted for many years the principal cargo sent back to England from the Colony. Another point—the size of the families. The mother of Governor William Phips had twenty-one sons and five daughters, and the Reverend John Sherman had six children by his first wife and twenty by his second. These were not uncommon figures in the early life of New England; and with so many numbers within itself the home life was a center for a very complete and variegated industrial life. Surely it is a long cry from these kitchen fireplaces—so large that often a horse had to be driven into the kitchen dragging the huge back log—these immense families, to the kitchenette and one-child family of to-day!

This, then, was the old Duxbury: the Duxbury of long, cold winters, privations, and austerity. Down by the shore to-day is the new Duxbury—a Duxbury of automobiles, of business men's trains, of gay society at Powder Point, where in the winter is the well-known boys' school—a Duxbury of summer cottages, white and green along the shore, green and brown under the pines. Of these summer homes many are new: the Wright estate is one of the finest on the South Shore, and the pleasant, spacious dwelling distinguished by its handsome hedge of English privet formerly belonged to Fanny Davenport, the actress. Others are old houses, very tastefully, almost affectionately remodeled by those for whom the things of the past have a special lure. These remodeled cottages are, perhaps, the prettiest of all. Those very ancient landmarks, sagging into pathetic disrepair, present a sorrowful, albeit an artistic, silhouette against the sky. But these "new-old" cottages, with ruffled muslin curtains at the small-paned, antique windows, brave with a shining knocker on the green-painted front door, and gay with old-fashioned gardens to the side or in the rear—these are a delight to all, and an honor to both past and present.

Surely the fair town of Duxbury, which so smilingly enticed the Pilgrims across the bay to enjoy her sunny beach and rolling pasture lands, must be happy to-day as she was then to feel her ground so deeply tilled, and still to be so daintily adorned with homes and gardens and with laughing life.

CHAPTER X

KINGSTON AND ITS MANUSCRIPTS

On a charming eminence at two crossroads, delicately dappled by fine elm shade and clasped by an antique grapevine, rests the old Bradford house. From the main road half a mile away you will see only the slanting roof, half concealed by rolling pasture land, but if you will trouble to turn off from the main road, and if you will not be daunted by the unsavoriness of the immediate neighborhood, you will find it quite worth your while. The house presents only a casual side to the street—one fancies it does not take much interest in its upstart neighbors—but imagination makes us believe that it regards with brooding tenderness the lovely tidal river which winds away through the marshes to the sea. Interesting as the house is for its architectural features and for its delightful location—despite the nearness of the passing train—yet it is on neither of these points that its fame rests.

In this house, built in 1674, and once belonging to Major John Bradford, the grandson of the Governor, was preserved for many years one of the most valuable American manuscripts in existence, and one fated to the most romantic adventures in the annals of Lost and Found.

Bradford's "History of the Plymouth Plantation" is our sole source of authentic information for the period 1606-46. It is the basis for all historical study of the early life of the Pilgrims in this country, and when we look at the quiet roof of the Bradford house to-day and realize how narrowly the papers—for they remained in manuscript form for two hundred years—escaped being lost forever, our minds travel again over the often told story.

The manuscript, penned in Governor Bradford's fine old hand, in a folio with a parchment back, and with some childish scribblings by little Mercy Bradford on the cover, passed at the Governor's death to his son, and at his death to his son. It reposed in the old house at which we are now looking until 1728, doubtless regarded as something valuable, but not in the least appreciated at its full and peculiar worth. When Major John Bradford lent it to the Reverend Thomas Prince to assist him in his "Chronological History of New England," he was merely doing what he had done many times before. In these days of burglar-proof safes and fire protection it makes us shiver to think of this priceless holograph passed from hand to hand in such a casual manner. But it seems to have escaped any mishap under Dr. Prince, who deposited it eventually in the library of the Old South Church. Here it remained for half a century, still in manuscript form and frequently referred to by scholars. Thomas Hutchinson used it in compiling his "History of Massachusetts Bay," and Mather used it also. At the time of the Revolution the Old South was looted, and this document (along with many others) disappeared absolutely. No trace whatever could be found of it: the most exhaustive search was in vain, and scholars and historians mourned for a loss that was irreparable. And then, after half a century, after the search had been entirely abandoned, it was discovered, quite by chance, by one who fortunately knew its value, tucked into the Library of Fulham Palace in London. After due rejoicing on the American side and due deliberation on the English side of the water, it was very properly and very politely returned to this country in 1897. Now it rests after its career of infinite hazard, in a case in the Boston State House, elaborately protected from fire and theft, from any accidental or premeditated harm, and Kingston must content itself with a copy in Pilgrim Hall at Plymouth.

Kingston's history commences with a manuscript and continues in the same form. If you would know the legends, the traditions, the events which mark this ancient town, you will have to turn to records, diaries, memoranda, memorial addresses and sermons, many of them never published.

It is rather odd that this serene old place, discovered only two or three days after the landing of the Pilgrims at Plymouth, is so devoid of a printed career. As soon as the Pilgrims had explored the spot, they put themselves on record as having "a great liking to plant in it" instead of in Plymouth. But they decided against it because it lay too far from their fishing and was "so encompassed with woods," that they feared danger from the savages. It was very soon settled, however, and remained as the north end of Plymouth for a hundred and six years, until 1726. Governor Bradford writes, in regard to its colonization:

"Y͡e people of y͡e plantation begane to grow in their outward estate ... and as their stocks increased and y͡e increase vendible, ther was no longer any holding them togeather, but now they must of necessitoe goe to their great lots: they could not otherwise keep catle; and having oxen grown they must have land for plowing and tillage. And no man now thought he could live except he had catle and a great deal of ground to keep them: all striving to increase their stocks. By which means they were scattered all over y͡e bay, quickly, and y͡e towne, in which they had lived compactly till now [1632] was left very thine, and in a short time almost desolate."

Governor Bradford seems to deplore this moving out of Plymouth, but as a matter of fact he was among the first to go, and his estate on Jones River comprised such a goodly portion of what is now Kingston that when he died he was the richest man in the Colony! A boulder marks the place which he, with that unerring eye for a fine view which distinguished the early settlers, chose for his estate. From here one catches a glimpse of water, open fields, trees, the Myles Standish Monument to the left, the sound of the passing automobiles behind. The distant smokestacks would be unfamiliar to Governor Bradford's eye, but the fragrant Kingston air which permeates it all would greet him as sweetly to-day as it did three hundred years ago.

Governor Bradford, who was Governor for thirty-seven years, was a man of remarkable erudition. Cotton Mather says of him: "The Dutch tongue was become almost as vernacular to him as the English; the French tongue he could also manage; the Latin and the Greek he had mastered; but the Hebrew he most of all studied." Therefore if the curious spelling of his history strikes us as unscholarly, we must remember that at that time there was no fixed standard for English orthography. Queen Elizabeth employed seven different spellings for the word "sovereign" and Leicester rendered his own name in eight different ways. It was by no means a mark of illiteracy to spell not only unlike your neighbor, but unlike yourself on the line previous.

But it is more than quaint diction and fantastic spelling which fascinates us as we turn over, not only the leaves of Bradford's famous history, but the pile of fading records of various kinds of this once prosperous shipbuilding town. The records of Kingston are valuable, not only because they tell the tale of this particular spot, but because they are delightfully typical of all the South Shore towns. The yellowing diaries mention crude offenses, crude chastisements; give scraps of genealogies as broken as the families themselves are now broken and scattered; lament over one daughter of the Puritans who took the veil in a Roman Catholic convent; sternly relate, in Rabelaisian frankness, dark sins, punished with mediæval justice. In fact, these righteous early colonists seemed to find a genuine satisfaction in devising punishments, and in putting them into practice. We read that the stocks (also called "bilbaos" because they were formerly manufactured in Bilbao, in Spain) were first occupied by the man who had made them, as the court decided that his charge for the work was excessive! There were wooden cages in which criminals were confined and exposed to public view; whipping-posts; cleft sticks for profane tongues. Drunkenness was punished by disfranchisement; the blasphemer and the heretics were branded with a hot iron.

Let us look at some of these old records, not all of them as ferocious as this, but interesting for the minutiæ which they preserve and which makes it possible for us to reconstruct something of that atmosphere of the past. It was ninety-six years after the settlement at Plymouth that Kingston made its first request for a separation. It was not granted for almost a decade, but from then on the ecclesiastical records furnish us with a great deal of intimate and chatty material. For instance, we learn in 1719 that Isaac Holmes was to have "20 shillings for sweeping, opening and shutting of the doors and casements of the meeting house for 1 year," which throws some light upon sextons' salaries!

The minute directions as to the placing of the pews in the meeting-house

(1720) contain a pungent element of personality. Major John Bradford is "next to the pulpit stairs"; Elisha Bradford on the left "as you go in"; Benjamin Eaton's place is "between minister's stairs and west door"; while Peter West is ingloriously, and for what reason we know not, relegated to the gallery "in the front, next to the stairs, behind the women."

It is significant to note (1728) that seats are built at each end above the galleries for the Indians and negroes.

Fish laws, rewards for killing wild cats, bickerings with the minister, and brief mention of the death of many women at an early age—after having given birth to an incredible number of children—fill up pages and pages.

The eye rests upon a resolution passed (1771) to "allow Benjamin Cook the sum of 8 shillings for a coffin, and liquor at the funeral of James Howland." They might not believe in prayers for the dead in those days, but there was evidently no reason why the living should not receive some cheer!

How is this for the minister's salary? The Reverend Doctor Willis (1780) is to receive eighty pounds a year, to be paid partly in Indian corn, rye, pork, and beef. Ten cords of wood yearly are allowed him "until he have a family, then twenty cords, are to be allowed, the said wood to be delivered at his door."

Mr. Levi Bradford agrees to make the whipping-post and stocks for nine shillings, if the town will find the iron (1790).

The wage paid for a day's labor on the highway (1791) was as follows: For a day's labor by a man, 2 shillings, 8 pence; for a yoke of oxen, 2 shillings; for a horse, 1 shilling, 6 pence; for a cart, 1 shilling, 4 pence. One notes the prices are for an eight-hour day.

However, the high cost of living began to make itself felt even then. How else account for the statement (1796) that Mr. Parris, the schoolmaster, has been allowed fifty shillings in addition to his salary "considering the increase in the price of provisions"?

There seems to have been a great celebration on the occasion of raising the second meetinghouse in Kingston (1798). One old account reads: "Booths were erected on the field opposite, and all kinds of liquor and refreshment were sold freely." After the frame was up a procession was formed of those who were employed in the raising, consisting of carpenters, sailors, blacksmiths, etc., each taking some implement of his trade such as axes, rules, squares, tackles and ropes. They walked to the Great Bridge and back to the temporary building that had been used for worship (the Quail Trap) while the new one was being planned. Here they all had punch and an "hour or so of jollity."

If the women's lives were conspicuously short, it was not so with the men. Ebenezer Cobb, who died in 1801 in the one hundred and eighth year of his age, had lived in no less than three centuries, having seen six years in the seventeenth, the whole of the eighteenth, and a year of the nineteenth.

The minister's tax is separated from the other town taxes in 1812—thus even in this little village is reflected the great movement of separation of

Church and State. In 1851 when we read of a Unitarian church being built we realize that the Puritan régime is over in New England.

Thus with the assistance of the Pelegs and Hezekiahs, the Zadocks, Ichabods, and Zenases—names which for some absurd and irreverent reason suggest a picture puzzle—we manage to piece together scraps of the Kingston of long ago.

We must confess to some relief at the inevitable conclusion that such study brings—namely, that the early settlers were not the unblemished prigs and paragons tradition has so fondly branded them. They seem to have been human enough—erring enough, if we take these records penned by themselves. However, for any such iconoclastic observation it is reassuring to have the judgment of so careful a historian as Charles Francis Adams. He says:

"That the earlier generations of Massachusetts were either more law-abiding or more self-restrained than the later is a proposition which accords neither with tradition nor with the reason of things. The habits of those days were simpler than those of the present: they were also essentially grosser...."

He then gives a dozen pages or so of hitherto unpublished church records, gathered from as many typical Massachusetts towns, which throw an undeniable and unflattering light on the social habits of that early period. As explicit and public confession before the church congregation was enforced, these church records contain startlingly graphic statements of drunkenness, blasphemy, stealing, and immorality in all its various phases.

There are countless church records which duplicate this one of the ordination of a Massachusetts pastor in 1729: "6 Barrels and a half of Cyder, 28 gallons of wine, 2 gallons of Brandy, and 4 of rum, loaf sugar, lime juice and pipes," all, presumably, consumed at the time and on the spot of the ordination. Even the most pessimistic must admit that long before our prohibition era we had traveled far beyond such practices.

The immorality seems to have been the natural reaction from morbid spiritual excitement induced by religious revivals. Poor Governor Bradford never grasped this, and we find him lamenting (1642): "Marvilous it may be to see and consider how some kind of wickedness did grow and break forth here in a land where the same was much witnessed against, and so narrowly looked on and severely punished when it was known."

We hear the same plaint from Jonathan Edwards a century later.

It is well to honor the Pilgrims for their many stanch and admirable qualities, but it is only fair to recall that the morbidity of their religion made them less healthy-minded than we, and that many of their practices, such as the well-recognized custom of "bundling," were indications of a people holding far lower moral standards than ours.

The old sermons, diaries, biographies, and records lie on dusty shelves now, and few pause to read them, and in Kingston no one yet has gathered them into a local history. There are other records traced, not in sand, but on the soil that may also be read by any who pass. Some remnants of the trenches and terraces dug by the quota of Arcadian refugees who fell to Kingston's share after the pathetic flight from Nova Scotia may still be seen—claimed by some to be the first irrigation attempt in America.

The old "Massachusetts Payth" which follows the road more or less closely beyond Kingston is traced with difficulty and uncertainty in Kingston itself, but there is another highway as clear to-day as it was three hundred years ago. And this is the lovely tidal river, named after the master of the Mayflower, up which used to come and go not only many ships of commerce, but, in the evenings after life had become less austere, boatloads of merry-makers from Plymouth and Duxbury to attend the balls given at what was originally the King's Town.

It has carried much traffic in its day, that river which now winds so gracefully down to the sea, and which we see so well from the yard of the old Bradford house. Down it floated the vessels made by Kingston men, and out of it was dug much bog iron for the use of Washington's artillery.

Monk's Hill—which the old records call Mont's Hill Chase, a name supposed to have been applied to a hunt in England—could tell a story too, if one had ears to hear. The highest land in Kingston, during the Revolution it was one of the points where a beacon fire was lighted to alarm the town in case of invasion by the enemy.

Kingston is not without history, although its manuscripts lie long untouched upon library shelves, and its historic soil is tramped over by unheeding feet. That the famous manuscript which was its greatest historical contribution has been taken away from it, is no loss in the truest sense of the word, for this monumental work, which belongs to no one place, but to the country as a whole, is properly preserved at the State House.

Kingston seems amenable to this arrangement, just as she seems entirely willing that Plymouth should claim the first century of her career. When one is sure of one's heritage and beauty, one does not clamor for recognition; one does not even demand a printed history. It is quality, not quantity, that counts, and even if nothing more is ever written in or about this dear old town, Kingston will have made a distinguished contribution to American history and literature.

CHAPTER XI

PLYMOUTH

One of the favorite pictures of New Englanders, and one which hangs in innumerable dining-rooms and halls, is by Boughton, the popular American artist, and is named "The Return of the Mayflower." I suppose thousands of New England children have gazed wonderingly at this picture, which, contrary to the modern canons of art, "tells a story," and many of those naïve minds have puzzled as to how those poor Pilgrims, who had no tea or coffee or milk or starch, managed to appear so well fed and so contented, and so marvelously neat and clean. The inexhaustible bag which inevitably appeared at crucial moments in the career of "Swiss Family Robinson" is nowhere mentioned in the early chronicles of the Plymouth Plantation, and the precise manner in which a small vessel of a hundred and eighty tons, carrying a hundred passengers, and all the innumerable cradles, chairs, and highboys which have since flooded the museums as "genuine relics" of that first voyage, could also have brought sufficient washboards, soap, and flatirons to have kept the charming costumes so immaculate is a mystery which will probably never be solved—especially since the number of relics appears to increase instead of diminish with the passage of time.

However, that is a mere trifle. Mr. Boughton, in catching this touching and dramatic moment in the history of the Plymouth Colony, has rendered a graphic service to us all, and if we could stand upon the little plateau on which this man and maid are standing, and could look out with them—we should see—what should we see?

We may, indeed, stand upon the little plateau—possibly it is no other than the base of Cole's Hill, that pathetic spot on which the dead were buried those first sad months, the ground above being leveled and planted with corn lest the Indians should count the number of the lost—and look out upon that selfsame harbor, but the sight which meets our eyes will be a very different one from that which met theirs. Let us, if we can, for the space of half an hour or so, imagine that we are standing beside this Pilgrim man and maid, on the day on which Mr. Boughton portrayed them.

Instead of 1920 it is 1621. It is the 5th of April: the winter of terrifying sicknesses and loss has passed; of the hundred souls which left England the autumn previously more than a half have died. The Mayflower which brought them all over, and which has remained in the harbor all winter, is now, having made repairs and taking advantage of the more clement weather, trimming her sails for the thirty-one days' return voyage to England. They may return with her, if they wish, any or all of the sturdy little band; they may leave the small, smoky log cabins; the scanty fare of corn and fish; the harassing fear of the Indians; they may leave the privations, the cramped quarters, and return to civilized life—to friends and relatives, to blooming English hedgerows and orderly English churches. But no one—no, not a single one returns! They have thrown in their lot with the new country—the new life. Their nearest civilized neighbors are the French of Nova Scotia, five hundred miles to the north, and the English of Virginia five hundred miles to the south. But they are undaunted. And yet—who can doubt that as they gaze out upon the familiar sails—the last banner between themselves and their ancestral home, and as they see them sailing out and out until they sink below the verge of sea and sky, the tears "rise in the heart and gather to the eyes" in "thinking of the days that are no more."

Three hundred years ago! The same harbor now as then, with the highland of Cape Cod dimly outlined in the gray eastern horizon; the bluffs of Manomet nearer on the right; opposite them, on the left, Duxbury Beach comes down, and ends in the promontory which holds the Gurnet Lights. Clarke's Island—already so named—lies as it does to-day, but save for these main topographical outlines the Plymouth at which we are looking in our imagination would be quite unrecognizable to us.

There is a little row of houses—seven of them—that is all. Log cabins, two-roomed, of the crudest build, thatched with wildgrass, the chinks between the logs filled with clay, the floors made of split logs; lighted at night with pieces of pitch pine. Each lot measures three rods long and a rod and a half wide, and they run on either side of the single street (the first laid out in New England, and ever afterward to be known as Leyden Street), which, in its turn, is parallel to the Town Brook. There is no glass in these cabin windows: oiled paper suffices; the household implements are of the fewest. The most primitive modern camping expedition is replete with luxuries of which this colony knows nothing. They have no cattle of any kind, which means no milk or butter; they have no poultry or eggs. Twenty-six acres of cultivated ground—twenty-one of corn, the other five of wheat, rye, and barley—have been quite enough for the twenty-one men and six boys (all who were well enough to work) to handle, but it is not a great deal to feed them all. At one end of the street stands the common house, twenty feet square, where the church services are held; the store-house is near the head of the pier; and at the top of what is now Burial Hill is the timber fort, twenty by twenty, built the January before by Myles Standish. In April, 1621, this is all there is to what is now the prosperous town of Plymouth.

And yet—not entirely. There are a few things left in the Plymouth of to-day which were in the Plymouth of three hundred years ago. If our man and maid should turn into Pilgrim Hall their eyes would fall upon some of the selfsame objects which were familiar sights to them in 1621. Those sturdy oaken chairs of Governor Carver, Elder Brewster, and Edward Winslow; the square, hooded wooden cradle brought over by Dr. Samuel Fuller; and the well-preserved reed one which rocked Peregrine White, and whose quaint stanchness suggests the same Dutch influence which characterizes the spraddling octagonal windmills—they would quickly recognize all of these. Some of the books, too, chiefly religious, some in classic tongues, William Bradford's Geneva Bible printed in 1592, and others bearing the mark of 1615, would be well known to them, although we must not take it for granted that the lady—or the man either—can read. Well-worn the Bibles are, however, and we need not think that lack of learning prevented any of the Pilgrims from imbibing both the letter and spirit of the Book. Those who could write were masters of a fine, flowing script that shames our modern scrawl, as is well testified by the Patent of the Plymouth Colony—the oldest state document in New England—as well as by the final will and various deeds of Peregrine White, and many others. The small, stiff baby shoes which encased the infant feet of Josiah Winslow, the son of Governor Winslow and destined to be Governor himself, are of a pattern familiar to our man and maid, as are the now tarnished swords of Carver, Brewster, and Standish. Probably they have puzzled, as we are still doing, over the Kufic or Arabic inscriptions on the last. The monster kettle and generous pewter plate brought over by the doughty Captain would be too well known to them to attract their attention, as would be the various tankards and goblets, and the beautiful mortar and pestle brought over by Winslow. But the two-tined fork they would regard with curiosity, for forks were not used, even in England, until 1650. The teapots, too, which look antiquated enough to us, would fill them with wonder, for tea was practically unknown in both colony and mother country until 1657. Those fragments of rude agricultural implements which we treasure would not interest our man and maid for whom they are ordinary sights, and neither would they regard with the same historical interest that moves us the bits of stone from the Scrooby Manor in England, the bricks from the old pier at Delft Haven in Holland, or the piece of carved pew-back from the old church at Scrooby. Possibly our Pilgrim maid is one of the few who can write, and if so, her fingers have doubtless fashioned a sampler as exquisite as that of Lora Standish, whose meek docility and patient workmanship are forever preserved in her cross-stitched words.

From all around the walls of Pilgrim Hall look down fine, stern old portraits, real and imaginary, of the early colonists. Modern critics may bicker over the authenticity of the white bull on which Priscilla Alden is taking her wedding trip; they may quarrel over the fidelity of the models and paintings of the Mayflower, and antiquarians may diligently unearth bits of bone to substantiate their pet theories. Our man and maid could tell us all, but, alas, their voices are so far away we cannot hear them. They will never speak the words which will settle any of the oft-disputed points, and, unfortunately, they will leave us forever to argue about the truth of the famous Plymouth Rock.

To present the well-worn story of Plymouth Rock from an angle calculated to rouse even a semblance of fresh interest is comparable to offering a well-fed man a piece of bread, and expecting him to be excited over it as a novelty. Bread is the staff of life, to be sure, but it is also accepted as matter of course in the average diet, and the story of Plymouth Rock is part and parcel of every school-book and guide-book in the country. The distinguished, if somewhat irreverent, visitor, who, after being reduced to partial paralysis by the oft-repeated tale, ejaculated fervently that he wished the rock had landed on the Pilgrims instead of the Pilgrims on the rock, voiced the first original remark about this historic relic which has refreshed our ears for many years. However, as Americans we are thoroughly imbued with the theory on which our advertising is based. Although it would seem that every housekeeper in the land had been kept fully informed for forty years of the advantages incident to the use of a certain soap, the manufacturers still persist in reciting these benefits. And why? Because new housekeepers come into existence with each new day. So, if there be any man who comes to Plymouth who does not know the story of Plymouth Rock, it is here set down for him, as accurately and briefly as possible.

This rock——which is an oval, glacial boulder of about seven tons—— was innocently rearing its massive, hoary head from the water one day in December, 1620, as it had done for several thousand years previously in unmolested oblivion. While engaged in this ponderous but harmless occupation it was sighted by a boatful of men and women——the first who had ever chosen to land on this particular part of the coast. The rock presented a moderately dry footing, and they sailed up to it, and a charming young woman, attired, according to our amiable painter, in the cleanest and freshest of aprons and the most demure of caps, set a daintily shod foot upon it and leaped lightly to shore. This was Mary Chilton, and she was promptly followed by an equally trig young man——John Alden. Thus commenced the founding of Plymouth Colony, and thus was sown the seed of innumerable pictures, poems, stories, and sermons.

Now the Pilgrims themselves, in none of their various accounts, ever mention the incident of the landing described above, or the rock. In fact they are so entirely silent about it that historians——besides discrediting the pretty part about Mary Chilton and John Alden, in the brusque fashion characteristic of historians——have pooh-poohed the whole story, arguing that the rock was altogether too far away from the land to be a logical stepping-place, and referring to the only authentic record of that first landing, which merely reads: "They sounded ye harbor & founde it fitt for shipping, and marched into ye land & found diverse cornfeilds & little running brooks, a place fitt for situation: at least it was ye best they could find." The Pilgrims, then, were quite oblivious of the rock, the historians are entirely skeptical concerning it, and the following generation so indifferent to the tradition which was gradually formulating, that in the course of events it was half-covered with a wharf, and used as a doorstep to a warehouse.

This was an ignominious position for a magnificent free boulder which had been a part of the untrammeled sea and land for centuries, but this lowly occupation was infinitely less trying than the fate which was awaiting. At the time the wharf was suggested, the idea that the rock was the actual landing-place of the first colonists had gained such momentum that a party was formed in its defense. An aged man, Thomas Faunce, was produced. He was ninety-five and confined to an armchair. He had not been born until twenty-six years after the landing of the Pilgrims; his father, whom he quoted as declaring this to be the original rock and identical landing-place, had not even come over in the Mayflower, but in the Anne. However, this venerable Canute, carried to the water's edge in his armchair, in the presence of many witnesses, assured them and all posterity that this was the genuine, undeniable landing-place of the Pilgrims. And from that moment the belief was so firmly set in the American mind that no power could possibly dislodge it. In accordance with this suddenly acquired respect, it was decided to move the huge bulk to the more conspicuous location of the Town Square. When it was lifted from its prehistoric bed, it broke, and this was hailed as a propitious omen of the coming separation of the Colonies from the mother country. Only the upper half was dragged up to the Town Square—a process which took twenty yoke of oxen and was accompanied by wild huzzahing. There the poor, broken thing lay in the sun, at the bottom of the Liberty Pole on which was flying, "Liberty or Death." But its career as a public feature had only begun. It remained in the square until 1834, and then on July 4 it was decided to drag it to a still more conspicuous place. So with a formal procession, it was again hoisted and hauled and set down in front of the entrance porch of Pilgrim Hall, where it lay like a captive mammoth animal for curious folk to gaze at. Here it was granted almost half a century of undisturbed if not secluded slumber. But the end was not yet. In 1880 it was once more laid hold of and carted back to its original setting, and welded without ceremony, to the part from which it had been sundered. Now all of this seems quite enough—more than enough—of pitiless publicity, for one old rock whose only offense had been to be lifting its head above the water on a December day in 1620. But no—just as the mind of man takes a singular satisfaction in gazing at mummies preserved in human semblance in the unearthly stillness of the catacombs, so the once massive boulder—now carefully mended—was placed upon the neatest of concrete bases, and over it was reared, from the designs of Hammatt Billings, the ugliest granite canopy imaginable—in which canopy, to complete the grisly atmosphere of the catacombs, were placed certain human bones found in an exploration of Cole's Hill. Bleak and homeless the old rock now lies passively in forlorn state under its atrocious shelter, behind a strong iron grating, and any of a dozen glib street urchins, in syllables flavored with Cork, or Genoese, or Polish accents, will, for a penny, relate the facts substantially as I have stated them.[2]

It is easy to be unsympathetic in regard to any form of fetishism which we do not share. And while the bare fact remains that we are not at all sure that the Pilgrims landed on this rock, and we are entirely sure that its present location and setting possess no romantic allurement, yet bare facts are not the whole truth, and even when correct they are often the superficial and not the fundamental part of the truth. Those hundreds—those thousands—of earnest-eyed men and women who have stood beside this rock with tears in their eyes, and emotions too deep for words in their hearts, "believing where they cannot prove," have not only interpreted the vital significance of the place, but, by their very emotion, have sanctified it.

It really makes little difference whether the testimony of Thomas Faunce was strictly accurate or not; it really makes little difference that the Hammatt Billings canopy is indeed dreadful. Plymouth Rock has come to symbolize the corner-stone of the United States as a nation, and symbols are the most beautiful and the most enduring expression of any national or human experience.

It is estimated that over one hundred thousand visitors come to Plymouth annually. They all go to see the Rock; most of them clamber up to the quaint Burial Hill and read a few of the oldest inscriptions; they glance at the National Monument to the forefathers, bearing the largest granite figure in the world, and they take a turn through Pilgrim Hall. But there is one place they often forget to see, and that is the harbor itself.

We began our tour through Plymouth through the eyes of a Pilgrim man and maid watching the departing Mayflower. It was the Mayflower, battered and beaten, her sails blackened and mended, her leaks hastily caulked, which was the first vessel to sail into Plymouth Harbor—a harbor so joyfully described as being a "most hopeful place" with "innumerable store of fowl and excellent good ... in fashion like a sickel or fish hook."

All that first dreadful winter, while the Pilgrims were struggling to make roofs to cover their heads, while, with weeping hearts, they buried their dead, and when, according to the good and indestructible instincts of life, which persist in spite of every calamity, they planted seed for the coming spring— all this while the Mayflower lay at anchor in the harbor. Every morning they could see her there; any hour of the day they could glance out at her; while they slept they were conscious of her presence. And just so long as she was there, just so long could they see a tangible connection between themselves and the life, which, although already strangely far away, was, nevertheless, the nearest and the dearest existence they had known. And then in April, the familiar vessel, whose outlines were as much a part of the seascape as the Gurnet or the bluffs of Manomet, vanished: vanished as completely as if she had never been. The water which parted under her departing keel flowed together. There was no sign on earth or sea or in the sky of that last link between the little group of colonists and their home land. They were as much alone as Enoch Arden on his desert isle. Can we imagine the emptiness, the illimitable loneliness of that bay? One small shallop down by the pier—that was the only visible connection between themselves and England!

I do not believe that we can really appreciate their sense of complete severance—their sense of utter isolation. And I do not believe that we can appreciate the wild thrill of excitement, the sudden gush of freshly established connection that ran through the colony, when, seven months later—the following November—a ship sailed into the harbor. It was the Fortune

bringing with her news and letters from home—word from that other world—
and bringing also thirty-five new colonists, among them William Brewster's
eldest son and Robert Cushman. Probably the greetings were so joyful, the
messages so eagerly sought, the flutter of welcome so great that it was not until
several days had passed that they realized that the chief word which Thomas
Weston (the London merchant who was the head of the company which had
financed the expedition) had sent them was one of reproof. The Mayflower
had brought no profitable cargo back to England, he complained, an omission
which was "wonderful and worthily distasted." While he admitted that they
had labored under adverse circumstances, he unkindly added that a quarter
of the time they had spent in discoursing and arguing and consulting could
have profitably been spent in other ways. That the first official word from
home should be one of such cruel reprimand struck the colonists—who had so
wistfully waited for a cheering message—very hard. Half frozen, half starved,
sick, depressed, they had been forced to struggle so desperately to maintain
even a foothold on the ladder of existence, that it had not been humanly
possible for them to fulfill their pledge to the Company. Bradford's letter back
to Weston—dignified, touching—is sufficient vindication. When the Fortune
returned she "was laden with good clapboards, as full as she could stowe, and
two hogsheads of beaver and other skins," besides sassafras—a cargo valued at
about five hundred pounds. In spite of the fact that this cargo was promptly
stolen by a French cruiser off the English coast, it nevertheless marks the
foundation of the fur and lumber trade in New England. Although this first
visitor brought with her a patent of their lands (a document still preserved in
Pilgrim Hall, with the signatures and seals of the Duke of Lenox, the Marquis
of Hamilton, the Earl of Warwick, and Sir Ferdinando Gorges), yet to us,
reading history in the perspective of three hundred years, the disagreeable
impression of Weston's letter outweighs the satisfaction for the patent. When
the Fortune sailed away it was like the departure of a rich, fault-finding aunt,
who suddenly descends upon a household of poor relations, bringing presents,
to be sure, but with such cutting disapproval on her lips that it mars the
entire pleasure of her visit.

The harbor was once more empty. I suppose that in time the Pilgrims half
forgot, half forgave, the sting of Weston's reproof. Again they gazed out and
waited for a sail; again England seemed very far away. So, doubtless, in the
spring, when a shallop appeared from a fishing vessel, they all eagerly hurried
down to greet it. But if the Fortune had been like a rich and disagreeable
aunt, this new visitation was like an influx of small, unruly cousins. And
such hungry cousins! Weston had sent seven men to stay with them until
arrangements could be made for another settlement. New Englanders are
often criticized for their lack of hospitality, and in this first historic case of
unexpected guests the larder was practically bare. Crops were sown, to be
sure, but not yet green; the provisions in the store-house were gone; it was
not the season for wild fowl; although there were bass in the outer harbor

and cod in the bay there was neither tackle nor nets to take them. However, the seven men were admitted, and given shellfish like the rest—and very little beside.

At this point the Pilgrims looked with less favorable eyes upon newcomers into the harbor, and when shortly after two ships appeared bringing sixty more men from Weston, consternation reigned. These emigrants were supposed to get their own food from their own vessels and merely lodge on shore, but they proved a lawless set and stole so much green corn that it seriously reduced the next year's supply. After six weeks, however, these uninvited guests took themselves off to Wessagusset (now Weymouth) leaving their sick behind, and only the briefest of "thank you's."

The next caller was the Plantation. She anchored only long enough to offer some sorely needed provisions at such extortionate prices that the colonists could not buy them. Another slap in the face!

Obviously, none of these visitors had proved very satisfactory. It had been entertaining under difficulties, and if the entertainers had hoped for the "angels unawares," they had been decidedly disappointed. Therefore it is easy to believe that they took fresh courage and sincere delight when, in July, 1623, the Anne and the Little James arrived—no strangers, for they brought with them additional stores, and best of all, good friends and close kinsfolk from the church at Leyden. Yes, the Pilgrims were delighted, but, alas, tradition has it that when they pressed forward in glad greeting to their old acquaintances, these latter started back, nonplussed—aghast! Like Mr. Boughton they had fondly pictured an ideal rustic community, in which the happy, carefree colonists reveled in all the beauty of picturesque and snowy collars and cuffs in Arden-like freedom. Instead they saw a row of rough log cabins and a group of work-worn, shabby men and women, men and women whose faces were lined with exposure, and whose backs were bent with toil, and who, for their most hospitable feast, had only a bit of shellfish and water to offer. Many of the newcomers promptly burst into tears, and begged to return to England immediately. Poor Pilgrims! Rebuffed—and so unflatteringly—with each arriving maritime guest, who can doubt that there was born in them at that moment the constitutional dislike for unexpected company which has characterized New England ever since?

However, in a comparatively short time the colonists who had been brought over in the Anne and the Little James—those who stayed, for some did return at once—adjusted themselves to the new life. Many married—both Myles Standish and Governor Bradford found wives among them; and now the Plymouth Colony may be said to have fairly started.

Just as a trail which is first a mere thread leading to some out-of-the-way cabin becomes a path and then a road, and in due time a wide thoroughfare, so the way across the Atlantic from Old England to New became more charted— more traveled. At first there was only one boat and one net for fishing. In five years there was a fleet of fifty fishing vessels. Ten years later we have note of ten foreign vessels in the harbor in a single week. And to-day, if the Pilgrim man and maid whom we joined at the beginning of our reminiscences could gaze out over the harbor, they would see it as full of masts as a cornfield is of stalks. Every kind of boat finds its way in and out; and not only pleasure craft: Plymouth Harbor is second only to Boston among the Massachusetts ports of entry, receiving annual foreign imports valued at over $7,000,000. Into the harbor, where once a single shallop was the only visible sign of man's dominion over the water, now sail great vessels from Yucatan and the Philippines, bringing sisal and manila for the largest cordage company in the whole country—a company with an employees' list of two thousand names, and an annual output of $10,000,000. Furthermore, the flats in the harbor are planted with clams, which (through the utilization of shells for poultry feeding, and by means of canning for bouillon) yield a profit of from five hundred to eight hundred dollars an acre.

No, our Pilgrim man and maid would not recognize, in this Plymouth of factories and industries, the place where once stood the row of log cabins, with oiled-paper windows. And yet, after all, it is not the prosperous town of to-day, but the rude settlement of yesterday, which chiefly lives in the hearts of the American people. And it lives, not because of its economic importance, but because of its unique sentimental value. As John Fiske so admirably states: "Historically their enterprise [that of the Pilgrims at Plymouth] is interesting not so much for what it achieved as for what it suggested. Of itself the Plymouth Colony could hardly have become a wealthy and powerful state. Its growth was extremely slow. After ten years its numbers were but three hundred. In 1643, when the exodus had come to an end and the New England Confederacy was formed, the population of Plymouth was but three thousand. In an established community, indeed, such a rate of increase would be rapid, but was not sufficient to raise in New England a power which could overcome Indians and Dutchmen and Frenchmen and assert its will in opposition to the Crown. It is when we view the founding of Plymouth in relation to what came afterward, that it assumes the importance which belongs to the beginning of a new era."

For this reason the permanent position of Plymouth in our history is forever assured. Old age, which may diminish the joys of youth, preserves inviolate memories which nothing can destroy. The place whose quiet fame is made is surer of the future than the one which is on the brink of fabulous glory. It is impossible to overestimate the significance of this spot.

The Old Coast Road—the oldest in New England—began here and pushed its tortuous way up to Boston along the route we have so lightly followed. Inheritors of a nation which these pioneers strove manfully, worshipfully, to found, need we be ashamed of deep emotion as we stand here, on this shore, where they landed three hundred years ago?

FOOTNOTES:

[2] It is hoped that by the summer of 1921 a beautiful and dignified portico of granite will be raised as a final and permanent memorial over the rock, which will be moved for the last time——lowered to as near its original bed as possible. This work, which has been taken in charge by the National Society of Colonial Dames of America will be executed by McKim, Mead & White. The General Society of Mayflower Descendants are also working for the redemption of the first Pilgrim burial place on Cole's Hill. The Pilgrim Society is to assume the perpetual care of both memorial and lot.

THE END

The Riverside Press
CAMBRIDGE. MASSACHUSETTS
U. S. A.

www.ingramcontent.com/pod-product-compliance
Lightning Source LLC
LaVergne TN
LVHW011126210726
843642LV00017B/719